# AUSTRALIA

## TRAVEL GUIDE 2025-2026

**Explore the Best of the Outback, the Coast, and Everything In Between – A Complete Journey Through Natural Wonders, Vibrant Cities, and Unique Experiences**

# **DISCLAIMER**

This travel guide is intended for informational purposes only. While every effort has been made to ensure accuracy, travel conditions, regulations, and services may change. Readers should verify important details such as visa requirements, safety guidelines, and local laws with official sources before traveling.

The author and publisher assume no responsibility for any losses, injuries, or inconveniences resulting from the use of this guide. Travelers are encouraged to exercise caution, use their best judgment, and adhere to local laws while exploring.

Any recommendations for businesses, activities, or services are based on research and opinions and do not imply endorsement. Always check with trusted sources for the latest updates before making travel decisions.

# TABLE OF CONTENT

# 1. Welcome to Australia

## 1.1 Why Australia Captivates Travelers

There are few places on Earth where red deserts meet turquoise reefs, where cosmopolitan cities rise beside sprawling national parks, and where the traditions of one of the world's oldest cultures exist alongside vibrant modern life. Australia is not just a destination. It's a world of its own. Stretching across nearly 3 million square miles, this sunburnt continent draws people in with its contrasts — lush rainforests and barren bushland, remote islands and buzzing urban centers, ancient landscapes and contemporary innovation.

Australia offers a sense of space that's difficult to grasp until you're standing in it. Travelers often describe the sensation as humbling. One moment, it's a salty breeze blowing across Bondi Beach as surfers chase the perfect wave. Next, it's the stillness of the Outback, where time seems to pause under a sky full of stars. It's this vastness that opens the door to wildly different experiences — sometimes within a single day.

The country's geographic diversity is matched by its cultural depth. Australia is home to the world's oldest continuous culture: the Aboriginal and Torres Strait Islander peoples, whose stories and connection to the land reach back over 60,000 years. At the same time, it's a nation shaped by migration. Italian cafes, Vietnamese bakeries, Lebanese delis, and Chinese night markets reflect just how globally entwined Australian life has become. In cities like Melbourne and Sydney, this multiculturalism is not just visible. It's part of the rhythm of daily life.

For travelers, Australia is a choose-your-own-adventure playground. Nature lovers drift toward the Great Barrier Reef or the Tasmanian wilderness. Surfers seek out Gold Coast breaks or the wild swells of Margaret River. City explorers roam laneways lined with street art and artisan coffee. Foodies track down farm-to-table dining in Adelaide or Indigenous flavors at a bush tucker experience in the Northern Territory.

Then there's the wildlife — strange and captivating. Kangaroos hopping across open plains, koalas clinging to eucalyptus trees, and platypuses swimming through creeks seem almost mythical to those seeing them for the first time. Australia doesn't just show its wild side in national parks. Even suburban areas can offer encounters with animals found nowhere else on the planet.

Adventure is practically a given. Whether it's hiking the Blue Mountains, snorkeling with manta rays in Ningaloo, sailing through the Whitsundays, or driving the Great Ocean Road, the landscapes invite exploration. But beyond the thrill, there's a grounded spirit of hospitality — a laid-back, straightforward warmth that makes people feel at home, even in the most unfamiliar terrain.

Each state and territory in Australia reveals a new side of the country. Queensland sparkles with reefs and rainforests. Western Australia offers rugged coastline and remote adventure. Victoria delivers style, sport, and a deep cultural heart. New South Wales hums with iconic sights and hidden coastal towns. The Northern Territory feels ancient and untamed. Tasmania, often overlooked, stuns with its purity and wildness.

Australia captivates not with one singular charm but with the balance between contrast and connection. Its identity is layered — raw and refined, ancient and current, welcoming and wild. That's why travelers keep coming back. There's always another path to walk, another beach to discover, another story to hear.

For anyone drawn to vast horizons and rich cultures, Australia doesn't just offer a trip. It offers a deep, memorable journey.

## 1.2 A Glimpse at the Culture, People, and Identity

Australia's cultural landscape is as layered and fascinating as its geography. At its core, the nation carries an enduring connection to the world's oldest living culture. For more than 65,000 years, Aboriginal and Torres Strait Islander peoples have passed down traditions, stories, and spiritual ties to the land that still shape how Australia is seen and understood today. Their influence is visible in sacred sites, art, music, and the Dreaming stories that explain the natural world in deeply symbolic ways.

In parallel, modern Australia reflects a rich blend of immigrant histories. Since the British arrival in 1788, waves of newcomers from Europe, Asia, the Pacific Islands, and the Middle East have brought new languages, flavors, and customs to the cities and regions they've called home. The result is a multicultural society where Italian espresso bars sit beside Vietnamese noodle shops, and Greek Orthodox churches share neighborhoods with Chinese temples. This blend doesn't just live in food and festivals—it's built into the rhythms of daily life, from how Australians speak to the way they celebrate community.

There's a distinctive personality to Australians, often described as friendly, laid-back, and irreverent. Humor is a national glue, and sarcasm is frequently used as a show of affection rather than offense. While there's a strong sense of fairness and equality, Australia also wrestles with the legacy of its colonial past. The conversation around reconciliation with Indigenous Australians continues to shape national identity, politics, and education. It's a topic that runs deeper than any tourist attraction, and engaging with it respectfully adds meaning to any visit.

In big cities like Melbourne and Sydney, a traveler might hear a dozen languages on a single tram ride. In the rural countryside or coastal surf towns, hospitality takes on a relaxed, informal charm. Across the country, shared spaces—from bush pubs to beach barbecues—create opportunities for easy interaction, where conversation flows without pretense.

Australia's identity isn't pinned to a single stereotype. It's equal parts ancient and modern, deeply rooted yet constantly evolving. Understanding this complexity gives travelers a richer view beyond kangaroos and koalas. It invites a more thoughtful exploration—one that listens as much as it looks.

## 1.3 Geography and Regional Diversity

Australia's geography is an epic study in contrast. From red desert plains to coastal rainforests, snow-dusted mountains to vibrant coral reefs, this landmass—roughly the size of the continental United States—unfolds like a continent of its own moods and rhythms. Sitting at the crossroads of the Pacific and Indian Oceans, it is a world shaped by millennia of natural forces and home to an astonishing range of climates, terrains, and ecological zones.

The majority of Australians live along the eastern and southeastern coastlines, where cities hug the beaches and lush hinterlands roll inland. This stretch includes Sydney and Melbourne, where urban life blends with proximity to surf beaches, leafy suburbs, and mountain ranges. The east coast is the most developed, with reliable public transport, highways, and coastal highways linking city to city. Further north lies tropical Queensland, known for its reef-draped shores and balmy climate, where sugarcane fields meet the Daintree Rainforest and the Great Barrier Reef spreads like a living mosaic just offshore.

In the south, Victoria and Tasmania bring a different energy. Cooler climates, alpine ranges, and art-forward cities define the region. Tasmania, in particular, feels remote and ancient, shaped by its convict past and rugged, untouched wilderness. Its national parks—Cradle Mountain–Lake St Clair among them—are havens for hikers and nature seekers craving solitude.

Traveling inland, the country changes shape. New South Wales and South Australia give way to arid plains and vast pastoral lands. As distance stretches, so does silence. The Outback begins not with a sudden shift, but a slow, creeping expansion where towns grow fewer and roads run longer. It is here that the essence of Australia's wild identity takes root. The Red Centre, anchored by Uluru and Kata Tjuta, offers not only geological wonders but a spiritual depth rooted in Aboriginal lore. In this region, the land speaks—through heat, color, and story.

The Northern Territory spans from desert to tropical savannahs. Darwin, with its balmy weather and crocodile-dotted waters, reflects a northern frontier mentality: laid-back but rugged. Indigenous cultures remain especially prominent here, with communities like those around Arnhem Land preserving traditions that stretch back tens of thousands of years.

To the west lies Western Australia, a massive region covering almost a third of the country's landmass but home to just a fraction of its population. Perth, its isolated capital, feels like a modern oasis separated by thousands of kilometers from the next major city. Beyond the city limits, the state reveals its hidden grandeur—emerald gorges, wildflower-covered deserts, and empty beaches that stretch without end. The Kimberley region in the north holds ancient rock formations, winding rivers, and the kind of remoteness that defines true wilderness.

Australia's coasts form a frame around its dramatic interior. The Great Ocean Road in Victoria twists and turns along sea cliffs and limestone stacks. The Nullarbor Plain stretches east to west in one of the world's longest, flattest expanses. The Coral Coast and Ningaloo Reef offer reef adventures far from the crowds, while southern coasts welcome whale migrations and windswept beaches.

Climate plays a large part in shaping each region's identity. While southern cities enjoy temperate seasons, the north experiences a wet-dry tropical cycle. Central Australia sees scorching summers and icy desert nights, while Tasmania endures crisp winters and mild, green summers.

For travelers, each region offers a distinct flavor. Some come to dive into the reef's warm waters, others to drive for days without passing another car. Whether navigating bustling city laneways or hiking a wind-battered ridge in the Outback, the experience is one of continual contrast and surprise.

Australia's regional diversity doesn't end with landscapes. It extends into language, customs, and even pace of life. City dwellers may move with cosmopolitan ease, while rural communities maintain a strong sense of grounded hospitality and local tradition. Indigenous languages, accents, and dialects still echo through place names and cultural events.

There is no single Australia. There are many. Each corner of the country contributes to its layered identity. Some regions feel ancient and untouched, others vibrant and contemporary. Yet all share a quality of space—openness not just in the land but in the way Australia invites exploration. It rewards those who linger, who look beyond the surface, and who are willing to travel far to understand what lies beyond the obvious.

From coastal cities to desert plateaus, alpine forests to remote island settlements, Australia's geography offers not only a map but a journey through extremes. These regions do not merely offer destinations—they shape the stories travelers take with them.

## 1.4 Quick Facts and What to Know Before You Go

Planning a trip to Australia comes with a few things to keep in mind. Whether the goal is to surf along the Gold Coast, hike through ancient rainforests, or wander the laneways of Melbourne, knowing a few basics makes the journey smoother.

Australia is both a country and a continent. It's the sixth-largest country in the world by land area, yet its population is just over 26 million. That means there's a lot of wide-open space between cities. Distances are vast, so travelers quickly learn that flying between major cities is common. For example, a road trip from Sydney to Perth would take several days.

The country is in the Southern Hemisphere, so the seasons are reversed from those in the Northern Hemisphere. Summer runs from December through February, while winter falls between June and August. Climate varies widely. Tropical regions in the north experience wet and dry seasons, while the south sees four distinct seasons. Inland deserts can swing between scorching days and chilly nights.

English is the official language, and the accent ranges in strength depending on the region. Australians tend to speak casually and with humor. Phrases like "no worries," "mate," and "arvo" (afternoon) come up often. It's a relaxed and friendly culture, though directness is appreciated.

Australia's currency is the Australian Dollar (AUD). Credit cards are widely accepted, but it's helpful to carry some cash when visiting smaller towns or markets. ATMs are easy to find in urban areas. Tipping is not required but is appreciated in restaurants or for exceptional service. A 10% tip is standard when leaving a little extra.

Power outlets run on 230V with type I sockets. Visitors from North America and Europe typically need plug adapters and voltage converters for electronics. Wi-Fi is widespread in cities but may be slower or unavailable in remote areas. Buying a local SIM card is a smart move for staying connected, with providers like Telstra, Optus, and Vodafone offering reliable coverage.

Australia is safe for travelers, but the natural environment demands respect. Beachgoers should always swim between the flags where lifeguards monitor conditions. In the bush, it's best to wear sun protection and carry water, especially during the hotter months. Venomous snakes and spiders exist, but encounters are rare and rarely dangerous if treated properly. Medical services are excellent in urban centers and regional hubs.

When it comes to entry, most travelers need a visa. The most common for tourists is the eVisitor or ETA (Electronic Travel Authority), both of which can be applied for online before arrival. A valid passport, proof of return travel, and sufficient funds may be checked at the border.

Time zones in Australia can be confusing. There are three main time zones: Australian Eastern Standard Time (AEST), Central Standard Time (ACST), and Western Standard Time (AWST), with variations during daylight saving time in some states. Sydney and Melbourne, for example, shift forward an hour in summer, while Queensland does not.

Cultural etiquette in Australia is informal. A handshake is the standard greeting, and casual attire is fine in most settings unless dining somewhere upscale. Respect for Indigenous culture is deeply important. Travelers will see Acknowledgement of Country signs, hear Welcome to Country ceremonies, and may visit sacred sites. It's essential to listen, learn, and follow any posted guidance when engaging with these areas.

In terms of accessibility, most cities have accommodations and attractions suited for travelers with disabilities, though rural areas may be less equipped. Public transport systems in places like Sydney and Melbourne include lifts, ramps, and support services.

Australia has a strict biosecurity system. Quarantine rules are taken seriously, so bringing in fresh food, plants, seeds, or animal products is highly restricted. Declare everything at customs, even if unsure. Penalties for undeclared items can be steep.

Local emergency services can be reached by dialing 000. This number connects to police, fire, or ambulance. Pharmacies are called "chemists," and medical centers are readily available, with many offering after-hours care.

In short, Australia offers a well-developed, exciting, and safe destination for travelers. Understanding a few practical details ahead of time helps remove the guesswork, so the focus can stay on the fun—from red desert adventures to tropical reef swims, there's something extraordinary waiting just around the bend.

# 2. When to Visit: Seasons and Regional Weather

## 2.1 Understanding Australia's Climate Zones

Australia isn't a one-season-fits-all kind of destination. Its climate shifts dramatically from the steamy tropics of the north to the crisp air of the southern coasts. Planning when to visit means thinking about what kind of adventure is calling. Want to soak up the sun on a golden beach? Go reef diving? Drive endless open roads under clear skies? Understanding the country's climate zones will help make it all fit.

Start with the basics. Australia has four main seasons—summer (December to February), autumn (March to May), winter (June to August), and spring (September to November)—but these don't play out the same way across the whole continent. In fact, it's more accurate to think in terms of climate zones: tropical, desert, temperate, and alpine.

In the tropical north, including places like Darwin and the Top End of Queensland, there are only two seasons—wet and dry. The dry season, from May to October, is the go-to time. Days are warm and sunny, skies stay clear, and humidity is low. It's ideal for outdoor adventures, wildlife spotting, and exploring national parks like Kakadu. The wet season, from November to April, means heavy rain, tropical storms, and high humidity. Travel is still possible, but some roads may close due to flooding.

Along the eastern coast, stretching from Brisbane down to Sydney and into Victoria, a humid subtropical climate takes over. Summers are warm to hot and can be muggy, especially around January. Winters are mild and sunny, with cooler temperatures further south. Beach towns stay lively year-round, but the shoulder seasons—spring and autumn—often bring the most pleasant mix of sunshine and comfort.

Southern Australia, including Adelaide and Melbourne, has a temperate climate. Expect warm to hot summers and cool winters, with temperatures dropping enough to need a jacket, especially in the evenings. This part of the country comes alive during the summer festival season, and in spring the countryside bursts with color.

Head inland to the Outback, and things get extreme. The desert climate means scorching daytime heat in summer and chilly nights, even below freezing in winter. For anyone aiming to road trip through the Red Centre or visit Uluru, cooler months from April to September make the journey more comfortable. Daylight is plentiful, and the air is clearer.

In the southeast, around the Australian Alps, winter brings snowfall and ski season to towns like Thredbo and Falls Creek. These alpine regions are the exception to Australia's usual sunny vibe and attract snow lovers from June through August. Spring and autumn still offer crisp hikes and changing scenery without the crowds.

When it comes to beach trips, the summer months shine—especially from December to February. But keep in mind, popular coastal destinations fill up fast, so early bookings and planning around school holidays help avoid the rush. Reef diving in the Great Barrier Reef is best from June to November when visibility is higher and stinger season is at bay.

Road trips, whether along the Great Ocean Road or across the Nullarbor Plain, benefit from shoulder seasons when temperatures are milder, and traffic thins out. Springtime wildflower blooms in Western Australia and autumn foliage in the Blue Mountains make those seasons worth considering.

Festival seekers will find events all year. Sydney's New Year's Eve fireworks are iconic, Melbourne hosts world-class food and culture festivals in March, and Darwin's dry season calendar is packed with local celebrations. From Christmas on the beach to Aboriginal art fairs and music festivals, every region has something special depending on the time of year.

As for daylight hours, summer brings long, sunlit evenings perfect for beach barbecues or watching kangaroos graze at dusk. In winter, expect shorter days—sunsets come early, particularly in southern states.

Humidity varies, too. Tropical regions like Cairns stay sticky year-round, while the Outback offers dry heat that's more bearable, even when the mercury rises. Coastal cities tend to have balanced conditions, with sea breezes keeping things tolerable.

Storms and weather events also factor in. Cyclone season hits the northern coasts between November and April, so it's wise to keep an eye on weather alerts if planning a trip to Far North Queensland or the Top End during that window.

Choosing the best time to go depends on what the trip is about. Want laid-back beach days and minimal rain? Aim for the southern coast in summer or the tropical north in the dry season. Chasing nature and wide-open landscapes? Visit the Outback in winter. Planning a culture-packed city escape? Autumn and spring offer perfect walking weather with fewer crowds.

Whatever the plan, there's a season that suits it. Australia's climate zones shape the rhythm of life and travel across the continent, and knowing them makes all the difference when building a trip that's memorable for all the right reasons.

## 2.2 Best Time to Visit by Region (Coast, Outback, Tropics)

Timing a trip to Australia often means planning around more than just seasons—it means aligning with the region's rhythm. Each part of the country moves to its own weather patterns, and understanding them can make or break an experience.

Along the eastern and southern coasts, where cities like Sydney, Melbourne, and Brisbane sit, the best travel window typically falls between late spring and early autumn. From October to April, days stretch long and warm, perfect for coastal walks, surf sessions, and seaside dining. December and January bring peak crowds and school holidays, so earlier spring or post-summer visits in March can be ideal for a quieter yet sunny adventure.

In contrast, the Outback calls for cooler months. Between May and September, central Australia offers dry, crisp weather that makes desert hikes and sunrise views at Uluru far more comfortable. Summer in the Outback often sees soaring temperatures well above 100°F, making outdoor activities intense and, at times, unsafe. Winter in the Red Centre, on the other hand, brings cool nights and pleasant days—ideal for road trips and stargazing.

Tropical regions in the north, including Darwin, Cairns, and the Top End, follow a distinct wet and dry season rather than four traditional seasons. The dry season, from May through October, offers the most accessible weather with lower humidity, blue skies, and minimal rainfall. This is the best time for exploring national parks, cruising through gorges, or swimming in waterfalls. The wet season from November to April brings monsoonal rains, afternoon storms, and occasional flooding. While it's lush and dramatic, it can limit access to remote areas.

Western Australia follows a blend of southern and tropical patterns. Perth and its coastal surroundings share the southern climate, with sunny summers and mild winters. But up north in Broome or the Kimberley, the dry season again reigns supreme, making May through September the most comfortable window.

Tasmania's weather leans cooler year-round. The summer months from December to February are best for hiking, wildlife viewing, and experiencing the island's festivals. Even then, packing layers is wise, as the island's weather can shift quickly.

For travelers seeking a mix of landscapes and climates, late spring (October to early December) and early autumn (March to April) strike the best balance across regions. These shoulder seasons often mean fewer crowds, mild temperatures, and greater availability for accommodations and tours.

Planning by region gives each traveler the chance to experience Australia at its most welcoming. Whether chasing sunlight on the Gold Coast or wandering through a cool eucalyptus forest in the Blue Mountains, knowing when each place shines can help shape a trip worth remembering.

## 2.3 Seasonal Events and Festivals

Australia doesn't just offer stunning beaches and iconic landscapes — it's a country that knows how to celebrate. No matter when the visit happens, something is always happening across its states and territories. From major arts festivals in the cities to quirky rural gatherings in the Outback, the calendar fills with events that reflect the diversity and spirit of Australia. Understanding the seasonal rhythm of these festivals will help shape the kind of trip that delivers both adventure and connection.

**Summer (December to February): Long Days, Big Celebrations**
If traveling during the Australian summer, expect a season brimming with energy, heat, and high spirits. This is the peak time for beach life, open-air events, and city-wide celebrations.

Start the year with **New Year's Eve in Sydney**. Watching the fireworks explode over the Sydney Harbour Bridge is one of the world's most iconic experiences. Booking well in advance is necessary, especially for rooftop dinners or harbor cruises.

In January, Australia comes together for **Australia Day (January 26)**. While the date stirs important national conversations, it's also a day of public events, concerts, and citizenship ceremonies. Sydney, Melbourne, and Brisbane host major gatherings, and coastal towns often feature community BBQs, boat races, and fireworks. For a different take, consider attending Indigenous-led events that offer a deeper understanding of the day's impact.

January also brings the **Sydney Festival**, one of the country's biggest cultural showcases. Over three weeks, the city bursts into life with theater, dance, music, and outdoor installations. Free events pop up around parks and squares, making it easy to stumble into the festival vibe.

**February** rounds out the summer with **Mardi Gras in Sydney**, especially the iconic LGBTQ+ parade along Oxford Street. This world-renowned celebration of pride, equality, and diversity attracts tens of thousands and spans weeks of parties, talks, and cultural events. Booking accommodations early in central Sydney is key during this time.

**Autumn (March to May): Harvest, Art, and the Quieter Side of Celebration**
As the weather cools and crowds thin, autumn becomes a beautiful time to explore regional festivals, particularly food events.

**Melbourne Food Festival** (usually March) is a feast for the senses. It spreads across the city and into the surrounding area . Expect everything from laneway tastings to high-end dinners with top Australian chefs. It's the perfect way to dive into the culinary culture without needing to leave the city.

In South Australia, **Tasting Australia** (typically late April into May) brings chefs, food lovers. Adelaide becomes a central hub, but events branch into regions like the Barossa and McLaren Vale, offering everything from foraging experiences to vineyard lunches.

**Moomba Festival** in Melbourne, held over the Labour Day weekend in March, is a family-friendly event with parades, live music, carnival rides, and the famous Birdman Rally — where participants launch themselves (and homemade contraptions) into the Yarra River.

This season is also known for **Adelaide Festival** and **WOMADelaide**, both held in March. These events turn Adelaide into Australia's arts capital for a few weeks. Think open-air performances, world music, experimental theater, and immersive art installations. The city becomes magnetic for culture lovers during this time.

**Winter (June to August): Cool Weather and Warm Celebrations**
Australia's winter is mild in most cities and makes the southern regions perfect for cozy, indoor festivals and alpine escapes.

Start in Darwin, where winter actually means the **Dry Season**, with sunny days and no rain. This is when the **Darwin Festival** (August) comes alive, offering outdoor concerts under the stars, art shows, cabaret, and multicultural performances. The laid-back tropical vibe mixes beautifully with this cultural explosion.

Further south, **Dark Mofo in Hobart** stands out. Held in June, this midwinter festival is unlike anything else in Australia. Run by the team behind MONA (Museum of Old and New Art), it blends eerie art, experimental music, and bold rituals — including a mass nude swim in the icy Derwent River. It's edgy, unforgettable, and very Tasmanian.

Winter is also the ski season in the Snowy Mountains and Victoria's Alpine Region. Festivals like **Peak Festival** in Perisher and **Snowtunes** in Jindabyne bring music to the mountains, mixing snow sports with DJs and bands.

**The Canberra Truffle Festival** (June to August) turns the capital's surrounding countryside into a gourmet playground. Truffle hunts, degustation dinners, and cooking classes fill the calendar, giving food travelers a reason to visit the cool southern landscapes.

**Spring (September to November): Blooms, Art, and Outdoor Magic**
As wildflowers bloom and temperatures rise, spring becomes a season of renewal — and one of the best times to attend both city and nature-driven festivals.

Start with **Floriade in Canberra**, the country's biggest celebration of spring. Held over four weeks starting in mid-September, the event fills Commonwealth Park with tulips, live music, food stalls, and night markets. Entry is usually free, and it's perfect for a picnic or a slow walk among thousands of blooming flowers.

**Sculpture by the Sea** (October to November) in Sydney transforms the Bondi to Tamarama coastal walk into a 2-kilometer outdoor art gallery. International and local artists install creative works along the cliffs and beaches, with the Pacific Ocean as a dramatic backdrop. Early mornings and weekdays are best to avoid crowds.

**Melbourne Fringe Festival** (September to October) brings independent theater, comedy, visual arts, and experimental performances to unconventional spaces around the city. It's edgy, grassroots, and great for discovering new voices in Australian arts.

**Planning Tips for Festival Travel**

- **Book Early**: Accommodations and domestic flights can fill up quickly around big festivals, especially in Sydney, Melbourne, Hobart, and Darwin.
- **Check Dates Annually**: Some events shift slightly each year, so it's important to confirm the calendar before booking.
- **Dress Accordingly**: Outdoor events might mean being exposed to Australia's strong sun or sudden weather changes. Sunscreen and a light waterproof jacket go a long way.
- **Embrace the Local Vibe**: Whether attending a big city gala or a small town fair, Australians generally approach festivals with a relaxed, open attitude. It's a great chance to strike up conversations and feel part of the community.
- **Combine Festivals with Travel Routes**: Many events happen in regions worth exploring before or after the main celebration. Turning a festival visit into a larger road trip works especially well in spring and autumn.

## 2.4 Packing Tips for Each Season

Packing for Australia means planning for a land of extremes. One day might start with a cool breeze in the Blue Mountains and end with a humid sunset in the tropics. Seasons vary across the country, and so do weather patterns between the coast, the Outback, and the alpine regions. Getting your packing list right will save time, space, and frustration—so here's a season-by-season guide to help figure out exactly what to bring and why it matters.

Summer (December to February): Hot, Humid, and High UV

If you're visiting during summer, pack with heat and sun in mind. Cities like Sydney, Brisbane, and Perth can be sweltering during the day but pleasant at night. Up north in places like Darwin and Cairns, humidity kicks in hard and the wet season brings sudden downpours. Sun protection is essential everywhere.

**Essentials to pack:**

- **Lightweight, breathable clothing:** Stick with cotton, linen, or moisture-wicking fabrics. Loose-fitting tops, shorts, and dresses will keep you comfortable.
- **Sun protection:** A wide-brimmed hat, UV-blocking sunglasses, and a high-SPF sunscreen are must-haves. The sun in Australia is intense even on cloudy days.
- **Swimwear:** Whether you're heading to Bondi Beach or the Great Barrier Reef, pack at least one swimsuit (two if planning multiple days near the water).

- **Quick-dry towel:** Useful for beach days, boat trips, or spontaneous swims under waterfalls.
- **Sandals and walking shoes:** Open-toed shoes or sandals are fine for cities and beaches. Lightweight walking shoes or runners are best for city exploring or short hikes.
- **Compact rain jacket:** If traveling to the tropical north, bring a thin, packable raincoat for afternoon downpours.

**Helpful extras:**

- Reusable water bottle (hydration is crucial in the heat)
- Insect repellent (especially in tropical regions)
- Portable fan or cooling cloth for humid days
- Light scarf or cover-up for sun protection or modesty at temples

Autumn (March to May): Mixed Weather and Layer-Friendly

Autumn is a great time to visit Australia—temperatures mellow, the skies stay clear, and crowds thin out. In the southern cities like Melbourne and Hobart, cooler mornings and evenings start to return. In the north, the weather becomes drier and more manageable.

**Essentials to pack:**

- **Layered outfits:** Think t-shirts or light long sleeves with a midweight jumper or fleece. You'll want to add or remove layers depending on the time of day.
- **Light jacket or windbreaker:** Morning breezes and evening chill are common, especially in coastal towns and the bush.
- **Comfortable walking shoes:** This is one of the best seasons for exploring vineyards, national parks, and city neighborhoods on foot.
- **Neutral-toned travel pants:** Stylish enough for city cafes, sturdy enough for rural areas.

**Helpful extras:**

- Scarf or neck warmer (lightweight but effective for wind)
- Umbrella or compact raincoat (especially for Melbourne where weather changes fast)
- Power adapter (check if bringing devices; Australia uses Type I plugs)

Winter (June to August): Cool to Cold Depending on the Region

While the idea of a cold Australia might sound odd, winter can bring frosty mornings, especially in places like Canberra, Tasmania, and the Snowy Mountains. Sydney and Brisbane stay mild, while northern areas like Darwin and the Kimberley enjoy dry, warm days.

**Essentials to pack:**

- **Warm layers:** A good-quality fleece or puffer jacket goes a long way. Add thermal undershirts or leggings if heading to alpine areas.
- **Jeans or thicker trousers:** Ideal for both city and country travel.
- **Weatherproof outerwear:** If going to the mountains, snowfields, or doing early-morning excursions (like whale watching), bring a rain- and wind-resistant coat.
- **Closed shoes or boots:** Opt for something warm and waterproof if snow or heavy rain is expected. Otherwise, a pair of good sneakers or ankle boots will do.

**Helpful extras:**

- Gloves, beanie, and scarf (especially in southern regions)
- Reusable heat packs or hand warmers (great for Tasmania or the Outback at night)
- Moisturizer and lip balm (the air gets drier in winter, particularly inland)

**Note:** Winter in tropical Australia (the Top End) feels like a mild summer elsewhere. Daytime temperatures hover around 25°C (77°F), so pack summer clothes and one lightweight jacket for evenings.

Spring (September to November): Blossoms, Breezes, and Mild Sunshine

Spring is perhaps the most comfortable season across the board. Days are long, rain is minimal, and nature is in bloom. It's great for road trips, coastal walks, and wildlife viewing.

**Essentials to pack:**

- **Light layers:** A short-sleeve base with a cardigan or light pullover is usually enough. Nights can be cool, but the sun warms up quickly by mid-morning.
- **Walking sandals or runners:** Comfort is key for long walks or day hikes.
- **Sun protection:** As the sun begins to intensify, bring that hat and sunscreen again.
- **Transitional outfits:** Midi dresses, long skirts, or rolled-up chinos work well for shifting temps.

**Helpful extras:**

- Camera or binoculars for wildlife and wildflower season
- Reusable shopping tote (markets pop up all over during spring)
- Allergy meds if sensitive to pollen (especially in rural areas)

Packing Tips by Region (Not Just Season)

- **Outback and desert travel:** Always bring a **wide-brimmed hat, fly net, strong SPF**, and **extra water capacity**. Nights can drop below freezing in winter, so a **thermal layer and sleeping bag liner** may come in handy if camping or glamping.
- **Tropical North:** Focus on **light, breathable clothes, mosquito repellent**, and **quick-dry gear**. A waterproof dry bag can protect electronics during boat rides or sudden downpours.
- **Coastal cities:** Pack a **versatile wardrobe**. Locals tend to dress casually, but dining out might call for one slightly dressier outfit.
- **Alpine regions:** If skiing or visiting during snow season, **thermal underwear, insulated gloves**, and **snowproof outerwear** are essential. Gear can be rented at resorts, but it helps to bring what you can.

General Packing Tips for Australian Travel

- **Luggage choice:** Soft-sided luggage works well for domestic flights or buses. A sturdy daypack is essential for outings and day tours.
- **Travel-size toiletries:** Larger bottles are unnecessary. Pharmacies are widespread and stocked with familiar brands.
- **Laundry options:** Most hotels and motels have laundry services or coin machines, so packing light is possible if planning to wash along the way.
- **Adapter plug:** Australia uses a Type I plug and 230V voltage.
- **Medications and prescriptions:** Bring any personal meds in original packaging and carry a doctor's note if possible. Pharmacies are well-stocked, but it's good to have essentials on hand.

Packing for Australia is about being smart rather than bringing everything. Pay attention to where and when the trip is happening, and adjust for layers, comfort, and functionality. The weather can shift quickly, and different states can feel like different countries at the same time of year. With the right mix of seasonal and regional gear, you're ready to take on coastlines, cities, bush tracks, and mountain trails without breaking a sweat—or catching a chill.

# 3. Getting There and Getting Around

## 3.1 International Gateways and Entry Requirements

Arriving in Australia is often the start of a long-anticipated adventure, but getting there takes some planning. The country is big—continent big—and once you land, understanding how to move around efficiently will shape the rest of your trip. This section lays out the best ways to enter the country, what paperwork to prepare, and how to travel once you're here. Think of this as a friendly walkthrough to avoid surprises and help you plan with confidence.

International Gateways: Where You're Likely to Land

Australia has several international airports, but most long-haul flights will land in one of the five major cities:

- **Sydney (SYD)**: Australia's busiest and most connected airport, with daily flights from Los Angeles, Singapore, London, Tokyo, and many others. A strong choice if your itinerary includes New South Wales or the East Coast.
- **Melbourne (MEL)**: Well connected to Asia, North America, and the Middle East. A great starting point for road trips in Victoria or for cultural travelers interested in food and arts.
- **Brisbane (BNE)**: Serves as a good entry for Queensland and the Great Barrier Reef. Flights from New Zealand, Asia, and the U.S. are frequent.
- **Perth (PER)**: Best if you're coming from South Africa, India, or the Middle East, or if you want to explore Western Australia.

- **Adelaide (ADL)** and **Cairns (CNS)**: Smaller, but increasingly used for international flights. Cairns is useful for reef-focused itineraries.

From the U.S., nonstop flights to Sydney and Melbourne are about 14 to 17 hours. From Europe, the trip often requires a layover in Asia or the Middle East. Major airlines like Qantas, Singapore Airlines, Emirates, and Qatar Airways are common carriers for inbound travel.

Visa and Entry Requirements: What You Need to Enter

Unless you're a citizen of New Zealand, you'll need a visa before arriving in Australia. The good news is, most travelers can apply online, and the process is relatively quick.

- **eVisitor Visa (Subclass 651):** For citizens of the European Union and a few other countries. It's free and allows stays of up to 3 months per visit.
- **Electronic Travel Authority (ETA - Subclass 601):** For travelers from countries like the U.S., Canada, and Japan. This can be applied for via the official Australian ETA app or website. It costs around AUD $20 and is valid for multiple short visits over 12 months.
- **Visitor Visa (Subclass 600):** For longer stays or if you're not eligible for the ETA or eVisitor. This has a longer application process and costs vary.

**Tip:** Apply for your visa at least two weeks before departure. While most approvals come through within 24 to 72 hours, delays can happen.

**At immigration:** Be prepared to show proof of onward travel, sufficient funds, and accommodation details. Australia is strict with customs—declare all food, animal products, and plant material. Failure to do so can lead to fines.

Clearing Customs and Biosecurity

Australia takes quarantine laws seriously. Items like fruits, seeds, honey, or even muddy hiking boots can be confiscated or cause delays. The safest route is to declare anything you're unsure about. You'll be given a form during the flight that asks specific questions about what you're carrying.

If you're bringing prescription medication, keep it in its original packaging with a doctor's note, especially if it contains controlled substances.

Getting Around Australia: The Big Picture

Once you land, getting around depends on your route, time, and travel style. Distances between cities are huge. A direct flight from Sydney to Perth takes about 5 hours.

Driving from Melbourne to Brisbane takes at least 18 hours. Planning travel across regions usually means combining flights, trains, and road trips.

Domestic Flights: Fastest for Long-Distance Travel

Domestic air travel is essential if you're visiting more than one major region. Australia's main carriers—Qantas, Virgin Australia, Jetstar, and Rex—connect all major cities and regional hubs.

**Tips for booking flights:**

- Book early for the best fares. Prices climb quickly, especially around holidays and school breaks.
- Budget airlines like Jetstar offer cheaper tickets, but baggage, seat selection, and even water may cost extra.
- Use Sydney or Melbourne as your base if connecting to multiple regions.

**Useful routes:**

- Sydney to Cairns (Great Barrier Reef access): ~3 hours
- Melbourne to Hobart (Tasmania): ~1 hour
- Perth to Broome (Kimberley region): ~2.5 hours

Trains: Scenic but Slow

Train travel isn't always the fastest, but it's ideal for slow travelers who value the journey. Two legendary train routes offer unforgettable experiences:

- **The Ghan**: Runs between Adelaide and Darwin through the Outback, stopping in Alice Springs and Katherine. It's a luxurious, multi-day ride with meals, tours, and sleeper cabins.
- **Indian Pacific**: Connects Sydney and Perth, crossing the entire continent in about 4 days.

These are bucket-list experiences, but pricey. Standard rail services also run between Sydney, Melbourne, Brisbane, and Canberra, but aren't as fast or frequent as in Europe.

**Tip:** If taking a long train ride, book a sleeper or premium seat and pack snacks, reading material, and headphones.

Driving in Australia: What to Know Before Renting a Car or Campervan

Australia is made for road trips, but you'll need to plan carefully. Roads are well-maintained, but distances are vast and services can be sparse in rural areas.

**Driver's license:** Visitors can drive with a valid license in English. If your license isn't in English, bring an International Driving Permit (IDP).

**Road rules to remember:**

- Drive on the **left side** of the road.
- Roundabouts go clockwise; give way to vehicles on your right.
- Speed limits are strictly enforced with cameras.
- Seatbelts are mandatory for all passengers.
- Watch for wildlife—especially at dusk and dawn.

**Best reasons to rent a car:**

- Exploring the Great Ocean Road, Tasmania, or the Blue Mountains.
- Traveling between small towns or national parks where public transport is limited.

**Campervans:** These are popular among long-term travelers. They're cheaper than hotels and offer freedom to explore remote areas, but parking and fuel costs add up.

**Road trip tips:**

- Always refuel before leaving remote areas.
- Download offline maps—some regions have no signal.
- Rest frequently on long drives; fatigue is a major cause of accidents.

Public Transportation in Cities

Australia's major cities have efficient, clean public transport systems. You won't need a car if you're spending time in Sydney, Melbourne, Brisbane, or Perth.

**Sydney:**

- Uses the **Opal card** for buses, ferries, trains, and light rail.
- Ferries are a scenic way to cross the harbor—great for reaching Manly or Taronga Zoo.

**Melbourne:**

- **Myki card** is required for trams, trains, and buses.

- The city's iconic **trams** are free within the central business district (CBD), making it easy to get around downtown.

**Brisbane:**

- Uses the **go card**, and has ferries along the river (CityCat), which double as sightseeing rides.

**Adelaide, Perth, Hobart, and Darwin** also have good local transport, but the systems are smaller.

Airport Transfers and Rideshares

Airport shuttles, taxis, and rideshare services like **Uber**, **Ola**, and **DiDi** operate in all major cities. Some cities offer train links directly from the airport (e.g., Sydney Airport to city center in 15 minutes).

**Tip:** Download rideshare apps before arrival and check airport signage for pickup zones—they're often separate from taxi ranks.

Booking Transport in Advance

While you can often book flights and buses on arrival, securing major travel legs before departure gives peace of mind and better prices. Use trusted sites like:

- **Skyscanner** or **Google Flights** for domestic flights
- **Rome2Rio** to compare travel modes
- **Greyhound** or **Premier** for intercity buses
- **Journey Beyond Rail** for The Ghan and Indian Pacific

Australia's scale can feel overwhelming at first, but once the logistics are clear, it all falls into place. By flying between distant regions and using trains, buses, or cars for local exploration, you'll get a complete picture of the country's rich landscapes and culture. Planning your movement is just as important as choosing what to see—and with a few smart steps, it becomes part of the adventure itself.

# 3.2 Domestic Flights, Trains, and Buses

Traveling within Australia takes some forethought. With a landmass roughly the size of the United States, getting from city to city or into the Outback often requires more than just a quick drive. This section walks through the most common ways to get around—flights, trains, and buses—and helps you choose what fits your itinerary, budget, and travel style. You'll see how each option opens up different parts of the country, from remote deserts to coastal hubs.

Domestic Flights: The Fastest Way to Cover Distance

When your trip spans thousands of kilometers, flying is often the most practical choice. Domestic air travel in Australia is frequent, relatively affordable, and covers all major cities and regional areas.

Airlines to Know

- **Qantas**: The national carrier with the broadest network and full-service offerings.
- **Virgin Australia**: Strong domestic coverage and solid service, slightly cheaper than Qantas.
- **Jetstar**: A budget airline owned by Qantas. Expect lower prices but extra fees for bags and seat selection.
- **Rex (Regional Express)**: Ideal for smaller towns, especially in New South Wales, South Australia, and Queensland.

Flights run frequently between big cities—Sydney to Melbourne sees dozens of departures daily. You can usually find affordable tickets if you book early, especially on budget carriers.

Key Routes

- **Sydney to Melbourne**: 1 hour 30 minutes, one of the busiest routes in the world.
- **Brisbane to Cairns**: 2 hours 30 minutes, great for reef access.
- **Perth to Darwin**: 4 hours, necessary for reaching the Top End.
- **Melbourne to Hobart**: Just over 1 hour, your link to Tasmania.

When to Book

- Book **2–3 months in advance** for the best fares.
- Midweek flights (Tuesday–Thursday) are typically cheaper.
- Budget airlines often run flash sales, so signing up for newsletters can pay off.

Baggage and Fees

- Budget carriers charge for everything: carry-on, checked bags, snacks, and even water.

- Full-service airlines like Qantas usually include at least 20kg of luggage and complimentary food.

Airport Locations

- Most airports are located 20–30 minutes from city centers. Some, like Sydney, are connected by train; others rely on shuttles or rideshare apps.
- In regional areas, be prepared for smaller terminals and fewer services.

Trains: For Scenic Travel and Unique Journeys

Trains in Australia are not designed for speed. They're built for the journey itself, offering a chance to take in landscapes that most people miss. For long distances, you're booking an experience, not just transport.

Famous Routes

- **The Ghan**: Runs from Adelaide to Darwin through the heart of the Outback. You'll stop in Alice Springs and Katherine for off-train excursions. It takes about **three days** and offers luxurious cabins, meals, and guided tours.

- **Indian Pacific**: Crosses the continent from Sydney to Perth. It's a **four-day** trip with sleeper cabins, restaurant service, and dramatic scenery, including the vast Nullarbor Plain.

- **Great Southern**: A seasonal route from Brisbane to Adelaide, combining coastal beauty and inland vistas over **three days**.

These long-distance routes aren't cheap, but they're considered iconic. Booking well in advance is essential.

Everyday Rail Services

- **NSW TrainLink**: Covers routes between Sydney, Canberra, Melbourne, and regional New South Wales.
- **V/Line (Victoria)**: Good for day trips from Melbourne to towns like Ballarat or Bendigo.
- **Queensland Rail**: Serves Brisbane to Cairns, including the **Spirit of Queensland**, which offers railbed seats for overnight trips.
- **Transwa (Western Australia)**: Runs limited services in WA, mostly useful for visiting towns near Perth.

Rail Pros and Cons

- **Pros**:
  - Scenic and relaxing.
  - More room than buses or planes.
  - Sleeper options on longer journeys.
- **Cons**:
  - Slow and less frequent.
  - More expensive than buses.
  - Delays are not uncommon, especially in remote areas.

**Tip**: Use trains if you want to take in the landscape, not if you're in a hurry.

Buses: Budget-Friendly and Great for Regional Access

If you're watching your wallet or want to explore smaller towns, long-distance buses (coaches) are a smart choice. They're not luxurious, but they are efficient, reliable, and cover more ground than trains.

Major Bus Operators

- **Greyhound Australia**: The largest and most flexible coach company, with passes available for unlimited travel. Great for backpackers and solo travelers.
- **Premier Motor Service**: Operates along the east coast, especially from Sydney to Brisbane.
- **Firefly Express**: Runs Melbourne–Sydney overnight routes.
- **Integrity Coach Lines**: Offers long-haul service in Western Australia, including routes between Perth and Broome.

Popular Routes

- **Sydney to Brisbane**: 16+ hours, with multiple stops along the coast.
- **Melbourne to Adelaide**: 10–12 hours, often overnight.
- **Brisbane to Cairns**: 24–30 hours depending on stops.

Most coaches are equipped with reclining seats, air conditioning, toilets, and Wi-Fi. Overnight trips save on accommodation but can be tiring.

Pass Options

- **Greyhound Whimit Pass**: Unlimited travel over 7, 15, 30, 60, or 90 days. Good for spontaneous itineraries.
- **Hop-on Hop-off Passes**: Choose a route and stop as you like along the way.

Booking and Boarding

- Book tickets online and arrive at least **15–20 minutes** early.
- Luggage is stored below, and a small carry-on is allowed.
- Bring snacks and water, especially for routes with limited stops.

When to Use What

| Scenario | Best Option |
| --- | --- |
| Crossing multiple states quickly | Domestic flight |
| Wanting scenic travel or a unique experience | Train |
| Budget-conscious with time flexibility | Bus |
| Regional travel between towns | Bus or regional train |
| Access to remote Outback areas | Regional flight or tour operator |

Combining Transport Modes

For longer trips, mixing transportation styles can offer the most rewarding experience. You might fly into Darwin, take **The Ghan** south to Adelaide.

Here's a sample combo:

- **Fly** into Brisbane.
- Take a **bus** along the coast to Cairns with beach stops.
- **Fly** to Uluru or Darwin.
- Finish with a **train** journey or return flight to Sydney.

This strategy lets you save time where needed but also slow down and enjoy the ride when it counts.

Booking Tips and Tools

- **Domestic Flights**: Use apps like **Skyscanner**, **Google Flights**, or **Qantas/Jetstar direct**.
- **Trains**: Check **Journey Beyond Rail**, **NSW TrainLink**, or **V/Line** for local tickets.
- **Buses**: Book via **Greyhound Australia** or **Premier's website** for the latest schedules.

Prices fluctuate, especially around school holidays and festivals. Book early during peak seasons (December–January and Easter).

In a country this vast, the journey between places can be just as memorable as the destination. Choosing how to get around is about balancing time, budget, and the kind of experience you're after. Whether you're staring out a train window at red desert landscapes, flying over the reef, or dozing on an overnight bus, movement in Australia becomes part of the story you'll tell.

## 3.3 Driving in Australia: Road Trips and Campervans

There's something freeing about hitting the open road in Australia. From winding coastal highways to dusty Outback tracks, driving lets you experience the country on your own schedule. You're not just getting from one place to another—you're discovering quiet beaches, forgotten roadhouses, and lookout points with no crowds. Whether you're behind the wheel of a compact rental or settling into a campervan for a few weeks, the roads here offer some of the most scenic and memorable travel experiences you'll have.

Why Drive in Australia?

Driving gives you the flexibility to stop where big tours won't and to follow your interests at your own pace. Some of Australia's best destinations—national parks, remote beaches, small towns—aren't always easy to reach by public transport.

Road trips are also woven into the culture. Australians often travel by car for long weekends, family getaways, or major holidays. You'll find well-kept roads, good signage, and plenty of places to stop for fuel or food, even in rural areas. That said, distances can be huge, and weather can shift fast, so smart planning is key.

What Side of the Road?

In Australia, people drive on the **left-hand side** of the road. The steering wheel is on the right-hand side of the vehicle. If you're coming from North America or Europe, it might take a day or two to adjust, but most drivers get the hang of it quickly.

Roundabouts are common. Yield to the right unless marked otherwise, and always follow posted speed limits, which are in kilometers per hour (km/h), not miles.

Getting a Driver's License and Insurance

Visitors can drive in Australia with a valid overseas license, but if the license isn't in English, carry an **International Driving Permit (IDP)**. Some rental agencies may require it, especially in rural areas.

Always include basic insurance with your rental. For campervans or longer-term rentals, consider additional coverage for windscreen damage, theft, and single-vehicle accidents. It might cost extra upfront, but it saves you a headache later.

Car Rental vs. Campervan: What's Right for You?

Car Rental

- Ideal for short trips, city-to-city routes, or day trips from major hubs.

- Available at all airports and in most towns.
- Choose a compact for urban travel or an SUV for national parks.

**Cost:**

Expect around AUD 50–100 per day, depending on car size and season. Fuel is priced per liter (average AUD 1.80–2.10 as of mid-2025), and most rentals use unleaded petrol.

## Campervan or Motorhome

- Combines accommodation and transport.
- Great for longer routes like the Great Ocean Road, East Coast, or Perth to Broome.
- Choose from compact 2-berths to full-size family vans.

**Popular rental companies:**

- **Britz**
- **Apollo**
- **Mighty Campers**
- **Jucy** (budget-friendly for younger travelers)

**Cost:**

Prices range from AUD 90 to 250+ per day depending on van size, features (kitchen, toilet), and season. Most companies offer unlimited kilometers.

## Top Road Trip Routes

Australia's roads were made for adventure. Here are some of the most iconic routes to consider:

### Great Ocean Road (Victoria)

- Length: ~250 km from Torquay to Allansford
- Highlights: Twelve Apostles, beach towns, rainforest hikes
- Best done in 2–4 days with coastal stops

### Pacific Coast (Sydney to Brisbane)

- Length: ~900 km
- Highlights: Byron Bay, Coffs Harbour, Port Stephens, Gold Coast
- Ideal for beach lovers and foodies. Takes 5–7 days or longer.

### Red Centre Way (Alice Springs to Uluru)

- Length: ~1,100 km loop
- Highlights: Uluru, Kings Canyon, MacDonnell Ranges
- 4WD recommended for some sections. Best in cooler months (May–September).

Tasmania's East Coast

- Length: ~300 km (Hobart to Bay of Fires)
- Highlights: Freycinet, Bicheno penguins
- Doable in 3–5 days, with excellent campsites and seafood.

Perth to Broome (Western Australia)

- Length: ~2,400 km
- Highlights: Coral Coast, Ningaloo Reef, Karijini National Park
- Remote but stunning. Allow 10–14 days.

Driving in the Outback and Remote Areas

If you're heading inland, especially in the Northern Territory or Western Australia, you'll need to be extra prepared.

- **4WD required** on some gravel roads and desert tracks.
- **Fuel up often**: stations can be 200–400 km apart.
- Carry **extra water**, a physical map, and an emergency kit.
- **Avoid night driving** due to kangaroos and livestock on the road.
- Mobile signals may be unreliable. Satellite phones or PLBs (personal locator beacons) are useful for remote treks.

Many rental companies restrict 2WD vehicles from unsealed roads, so check your rental agreement carefully.

Campgrounds and Free Camping

If you're traveling in a campervan, Australia is well set up with both paid campgrounds and free camping options.

Paid Holiday Parks

- Powered and unpowered sites
- Showers, laundry, cooking areas
- Cost: AUD 25–50 per night
- Examples: BIG4 Holiday Parks, Discovery Parks

National Park Campgrounds

- Often more basic (pit toilets, no power)
- Reservations may be required during peak season
- Cost: AUD 10–30 per night

Free Camping

- Available in some rural towns and designated roadside areas
- Must be self-contained (toilet, grey water tank)
- Use apps like **WikiCamps** or **CamperMate** to find locations

Always check signage before parking overnight. Fines for illegal camping can be steep in coastal and urban zones.

Fueling Up and Driving Distances

Australia is big—really big. What looks close on a map can easily be a **5-hour drive** or more.

**Fuel types**:

- **Unleaded (91)**: standard petrol
- **Diesel**: common for larger vehicles and 4WDs
- **Premium** (95/98): required by some rentals

Fuel costs vary by region. Remote Outback stations charge significantly more. Pay attention to signs warning "Next fuel: 300 km" and don't push your luck.

Driving Rules and Tips

- **Seatbelts** are mandatory for all passengers.
- **No phone use** while driving (unless hands-free).
- **Drink driving limits** are strict—0.05% BAC in most states.
- Watch for **wildlife**—kangaroos, wombats, and emus can jump into the road unexpectedly.
- Use **headlights** in rural areas and during dusk/dawn even in daylight.
- Pull over at **designated rest stops** every couple of hours. Fatigue-related accidents are a serious risk.

Rental Tips and Travel Insurance

- Compare rental agencies through sites like **VroomVroomVroom** or **Rentalcars.com**.
- One-way rentals often carry a drop-off fee—factor that into your budget.
- Check if your **travel insurance** covers rental cars or campervans. It may be cheaper than buying excess insurance at the counter.

Driving in Australia isn't just a way to get around. It's part of the journey itself. From quiet Outback roads to cliff-hugging coastal drives, there's a kind of solitude and wonder you don't get on public transport. With the windows down, a playlist rolling, and endless space ahead, you're not just going to your next stop. You're living the road trip story you'll talk about long after the trip is over.

## 3.4 Public Transport and City Travel Tips

Getting around Australia's cities without driving is often more convenient than expected. Public transport is well-integrated in major cities like Sydney, Melbourne, Brisbane, and Perth. You'll find buses, trains, trams, and ferries all accessible with prepaid cards or contactless payments. Once you understand how each system works, getting around becomes smooth, cost-effective, and surprisingly enjoyable.

Sydney: Trains, Ferries, and Buses

**Opal Card**
 To ride trains, buses, ferries, and light rail in Sydney, pick up an **Opal card** (or use a contactless debit/credit card). The Opal system offers daily, weekly, and Sunday fare caps, which help keep costs in check.

- **Daily Cap**: AU$17.80
- **Weekly Cap**: AU$50
- **Sunday Cap**: AU$8.90

**Costs by Mode** (as of July 2025):

- **Train** (CBD to suburbs): AU$4.00–AU$8.50 depending on distance
- **Ferry** (Circular Quay to Manly): AU$8.04 with Opal
- **Light Rail/Bus**: AU$3.20–AU$4.60

**Tips**
 Use the **TripView** app for real-time transport updates. Tap on and tap off for correct fares. Trains and ferries offer beautiful scenic rides—especially the ferry from Circular Quay.

Melbourne: Tram Heaven and myki Cards

Melbourne's trams are iconic and easy to use. You'll need a **myki card** for trams, buses, and trains, available at 7-Eleven stores and stations.

### Free Tram Zone

The CBD offers a **Free Tram Zone**—no payment or card required. This includes popular spots like Federation Square, Bourke Street Mall, and Docklands.

### myki Pass Prices:

- **2-Hour Fare**: AU$5.30 (full), AU$2.65 (concession)
- **Daily Cap**: AU$10.60
- **7-Day Pass**: AU$53.00

### Tips

Top up before boarding, and always touch on. Use the **PTV app** to find the quickest tram route or track delays. Buses are more useful for reaching suburbs or outer attractions.

Brisbane: Buses, Trains, and River Cats

In Brisbane, public transit is efficient and scenic, especially on the river.

### go card

Grab a **go card** at the airport, major stations, or 7-Eleven. It works for **buses, trains, ferries, and the CityCat river catamarans**.

### Costs (go card rates):

- **Peak Travel**: AU$3.63–AU$6.25
- **Off-Peak**: AU$2.90–AU$5.00
- **CityCat Ferry (short trip)**: Around AU$3.50

### Tips

There's a 20% discount for off-peak travel. Download the **TransLink app** for schedules. The **CityHopper ferry** offers free rides across key downtown stops.

Perth: SmartRider Cards and Free CAT Buses

Perth's system is clean and affordable, with one major bonus: **free buses** in the CBD.

## SmartRider Card

Use for buses, trains, and ferries. Cards are AU$10 (including AU$5 credit) and can be topped up online or in-person.

**Typical Fares**:

- **2-zone trip** (e.g., city to Fremantle): AU$3.20
- **Daily Cap**: AU$9.60
- **CAT Buses**: Free in the city and Fremantle

## Tips

Download the **Transperth app**. Trains are best for long-distance day trips (e.g., Fremantle or Rockingham), while buses connect inner-city stops and beaches.

## Adelaide: MetroCard and Beach-to-City Trams

Compact and efficient, Adelaide is great for short public transport hops.

## MetroCard

Works across buses, trains, and trams. Get one at stations or convenience stores.

**Fares** (MetroCard off-peak/peak):

- **Single trip**: AU$2.10–AU$4.00
- **Daily Cap**: AU$10.60
- **Tram (within city loop)**: Free

## Tips

The **Free City Connector bus** makes loops through major downtown stops. Glenelg Beach is reachable via tram in about 25 minutes.

## Canberra: MyWay Cards and Light Rail

Australia's capital has grown its light rail network and maintains a reliable bus system.

## MyWay Card

Use for both **buses and light rail**. Available at newsagents, MyWay agents, and stations.

**Fares** (standard adult):

- **Peak**: AU$3.22
- **Off-peak**: AU$2.55
- **Daily Cap**: AU$9.60

**Tips**

Use the **Transport Canberra app** to plan routes and manage top-ups. Most tourist destinations are within one or two zones.

Hobart, Darwin, and Smaller Cities

Public transport in smaller cities and towns is limited but functional for short stays.

### Hobart (Metro Tasmania)

- Buses only, fares range from AU$3.20 to AU$5.40
- Best to get a **Greencard** for discounts (up to 20%)
- Most useful for airport access and traveling to MONA museum

### Darwin

- Bus tickets: AU$3.00 (2-hour pass)
- Weekly passes: AU$20.00
- No train or tram system available
- Use for city center, Nightcliff, Casuarina, and the Museum & Art Gallery

In smaller towns or tourist-heavy regions like Alice Springs or Cairns, renting a car or joining local tours may be more practical.

General Public Transport Tips and Budget Insights

### 1. Ticketing Systems

Each city uses its own contactless card: Opal (Sydney), myki (Melbourne), go card (Brisbane), SmartRider (Perth), MetroCard (Adelaide), and MyWay (Canberra). Be sure to get the right one for each city. These can often be used on multiple modes of transport—bus, train, ferry.

### 2. Average Daily Budget for Public Transit

- **Light Users (1–2 rides/day)**: AU$5–AU$10
- **Frequent Travelers (3–5 rides/day)**: AU$10–AU$15
- **Weekly Transit Budget**: AU$50–AU$70 depending on city and distance

### 3. Airport Transfers

Airport links vary:

- **Sydney**: AU$18.74 one-way by train from airport to CBD
- **Melbourne**: AU$20.00 SkyBus (no train)
- **Brisbane**: AU$19.50 Airtrain (airport to city)

- **Perth**: AU$4.90 public bus or AU$12 shuttle

## 4. Useful Apps

- **Google Maps** works across cities
- Local apps: TripView (Sydney), PTV (Melbourne), TransLink (Brisbane), Transperth (Perth), Moovit (Adelaide), and Transport Canberra

## 5. Accessibility and Safety

Most modern buses and trains are wheelchair-accessible. Security is generally good, though late-night services can be sparse.

## 6. Tapping Rules

Always tap on and off where required, or you'll get charged the maximum fare. Some trams and buses (especially in Melbourne's Free Zone) don't require tap-on.

Public transport in Australia is more than just a way to get from A to B. It's often part of the experience—from ferry views of Sydney Harbour to a tram rattling past Melbourne's cafés. With a bit of planning and the right card in your pocket, it becomes a reliable, budget-friendly, and surprisingly scenic way to explore the country's urban hubs.

# 4. Where to Stay: Accommodation Options

## 4.1 Hotels, Resorts, and City Apartments

Finding the right place to stay in Australia can shape your entire trip. Whether it's waking up to skyline views in a Sydney high-rise or falling asleep to waves lapping outside a beachfront cabin, there's a wide spread of options here to suit nearly every budget and style. Some travelers prefer sleek city apartments for their independence and kitchen access, while others lean into the comfort and convenience of full-service hotels. Then there are the nature lovers, choosing rustic farmstays, eco-lodges, or quiet motels on the edge of a rainforest. You'll find that where you stay often becomes part of the story you tell later.

City Hotels and Serviced Apartments

In cities like Sydney, Melbourne, Brisbane, and Perth, the most common accommodation types are **hotels**, **serviced apartments**, and **boutique lodgings**. Chain hotels like Novotel, Hilton, Sofitel, and Ibis are readily available, especially in central business districts and airport zones. These typically offer modern comforts like in-room Wi-Fi, air conditioning, on-site dining, and sometimes pools or gyms. What makes them appealing is predictability—you know what you're getting.

If you're planning to stay for several nights or want a little more breathing room, **serviced apartments** are worth considering. These are furnished studio or one-bedroom apartments (often in buildings like Meriton Suites, Adina, or Quest) with full kitchens, laundry machines, and more privacy. They're ideal for couples, business travelers, or families who want flexibility to cook and relax.

## Average Prices (as of July 2025):

- Budget hotel (2–3 stars): AU$90–AU$150/night
- Mid-range hotel (3–4 stars): AU$160–AU$250/night
- High-end hotel (5 stars): AU$300–AU$600+/night
- Serviced apartment: AU$180–AU$350/night (depends on location and size)

## Where to Book:
Try platforms like **Booking.com**, **Hotels.com**, **Expedia**, and **Agoda**. These usually offer free cancellation and helpful maps to gauge location. **Airbnb** is widely used in Australian cities, but be aware that cleaning fees can inflate the cost.

## Tips:
Stay near major transport hubs if you're planning lots of sightseeing. In Sydney, look at Circular Quay, Darling Harbour, or Surry Hills. In Melbourne, check out Southbank or Carlton for quick tram access and local flavor.

Beach Resorts and Coastal Getaways

If waking up to the sound of the ocean is your thing, Australia's coast delivers in spades. From the laid-back shores of Byron Bay to the luxury of Queensland's Whitsundays, **beach resorts** run the full spectrum. In tourist-heavy zones like Gold Coast or Noosa, resorts are polished and spacious, often offering private beach access, infinity pools, spas, and in-house restaurants.

In smaller surf towns and hidden bays, the accommodations get more casual. Think of low-rise motels, beach cottages, or **eco-resorts** nestled among sand dunes. These spots are more about vibe than glitz, with surfboards out front and hammocks in the trees.

## Price Ranges:

- Beach motel or cabin: AU$120–AU$200/night
- Mid-range coastal resort: AU$220–AU$400/night

- Luxury coastal resort: AU$500–AU$1000+/night (especially near the Great Barrier Reef or Margaret River)

**When to Book:**

Prices spike during **school holidays (December–January)** and **Easter**, particularly near beaches. Booking 3–6 months ahead is smart if you're eyeing high-demand areas like Byron, Port Douglas, or Freycinet.

Eco-Lodges, Farmstays, and Rural Retreats

Outside the cities and off the main highways, accommodations often reflect the landscape itself. In the hinterlands, **farmstays** and **eco-lodges** offer more than a bed—they provide a sense of place. You might stay on a working cattle station in Queensland, pick your breakfast eggs from a henhouse, or spend nights under the stars in a solar-powered cottage.

**Eco-lodges** focus on sustainability, often using rainwater tanks, compost toilets, and passive design. These can be luxurious or rustic, depending on the region. Tasmania, the Blue Mountains, and Far North Queensland have a growing number of these earthy getaways.

**Farmstays**, especially in Victoria and South Australia, are great for families and often include animal feeding, orchard walks, and homemade meals.

**Typical Costs:**

- Rustic cabin or bush lodge: AU$110–AU$200/night
- Mid-range eco-lodge or farmstay: AU$220–AU$350/night
- Luxury eco-retreats: AU$500+/night

**Platforms to Use:**

Look at **Riparide**, **Airbnb**, or **Youcamp/Hipcamp Australia** for more off-grid, private listings.

Backpacker Hostels and Budget Options

For shoestring travelers or those seeking social atmospheres, **hostels** still play a big role in Australia. They're especially common along the east coast (Sydney to Cairns), and in cities, they often have great locations and community events. Options range from basic bunk rooms to clean and modern hostels with rooftop bars and coworking spaces.

Even if you're not the bunk-bed type, many hostels offer **private rooms** with en suite bathrooms. This gives you affordability without sacrificing comfort.

**Average Costs:**

- Dorm bed (6–12 people): AU$30–AU$60/night
- Private room in hostel: AU$80–AU$130/night

**Where to Book:**
Try **Hostelworld, YHA Australia,** or **Booking.com**. Hostels like Wake Up! (Sydney), Bounce (Melbourne), and Gilligan's (Cairns) are popular with both solo travelers and groups.

Camping, Cabins, and Holiday Parks

Australia is a paradise for campers. Whether you're pitching a tent near the beach, renting a cabin by a river, or pulling up in a campervan, **holiday parks** and **campgrounds** are widely available. These often include shared kitchens, BBQ pits, laundry, and clean restrooms.

Cabins at holiday parks are great for families or road trippers who want a budget-friendly bed without roughing it. They're usually basic but clean, with private bathrooms and kitchenettes.

**Costs:**

- Powered campsite: AU$25–AU$50/night
- Unpowered tent site: AU$15–AU$30/night
- Cabin: AU$80–AU$180/night

**Popular Sites:**
Check **BIG4 Holiday Parks**, **Discovery Parks**, and **Hipcamp** for unique stays in national parks or private land. National parks often require advance permits.

Seasonal Pricing and Booking Tips

Accommodation prices in Australia swing based on season, location, and event calendars.

- **Peak Season**: December–January (summer holidays), Easter week, school breaks
- **Shoulder Season**: March–May, September–November
- **Low Season**: June–August (winter, especially in southern states)

Booking platforms often offer **free cancellation** and **last-minute deals**, but popular areas like Uluru, the Whitsundays, and the Great Ocean Road tend to fill quickly, especially for boutique and family-friendly stays.

Amenities and What to Expect

Across most accommodations, you'll find Wi-Fi, air conditioning (except in remote eco stays), and tea/coffee facilities. In high-end hotels, you can expect breakfast buffets, concierge service, and sometimes airport transfers. In apartments, expect laundry machines and cooking gear. Hosts and owners tend to be friendly, happy to recommend restaurants or help book tours.

If you're staying rural, you may need to bring supplies like groceries or fuel. Some eco-lodges rely on solar power, so pack accordingly (no hair dryers). Always read recent reviews to check for hidden fees or location quirks.

Australia's variety of places to stay lets you mix things up throughout your trip. Spend a few nights in a Sydney high-rise, then unwind at a cabin by the beach or sleep among gum trees in a rainforest lodge. No matter your style or budget, there's a spot waiting with a view—and a story.

# 4.2 Unique Stays: Eco-Lodges, Farmstays, and Remote Cabins

If you're looking for something beyond hotel lobbies and apartment towers, Australia delivers in quiet, memorable ways. The country's wide open spaces are dotted with unique stays that put you closer to nature, people, and the land itself. Whether it's a solar-powered cabin deep in the bush, a working farm that serves homemade bread in the morning, or a timber eco-lodge perched above a rainforest canopy, these places don't just offer a bed—they shape the way the trip feels.

Choosing a unique stay doesn't mean giving up comfort. Many of these properties are beautifully designed and thoughtfully run. Some lean rustic, with simple furnishings and outdoor showers under the stars. Others offer luxury in unexpected places, like private hot tubs facing snow-capped peaks or fire pits glowing beside desert dunes. The beauty of these stays lies in how they connect you to the landscape and community around you.

Eco-Lodges: Where Comfort Meets Sustainability

Eco-lodges are growing across Australia, especially in areas like Tasmania, Queensland's Daintree Rainforest, and parts of Victoria's Great Ocean Road. These properties are built with environmental care in mind. You might notice solar panels, composting toilets, recycled timber, and water-saving systems. But you'll also find warm beds, handmade soaps, and views that stop you in your tracks.

In Queensland's Daintree, for example, lodges sit within World Heritage rainforest, where guests fall asleep to frog calls and wake to birdsong. In Tasmania's Bay of Fires, cliffside pavilions offer floor-to-ceiling windows facing the Southern Ocean, all designed to leave the smallest possible footprint. These stays work well for couples, solo travelers, or small families looking for a quieter experience that's more rooted in place.

**Average Costs:**

- Mid-range eco-lodges: AU$220–AU$400 per night
- High-end eco-retreats: AU$500–AU$1200+ per night (depending on season and exclusivity)

**Booking Notes:**
Check sites like **EcoRetreats Australia**, **Riparide**, or **Airbnb (filtered by 'unique stays')**. Many of these lodges have limited rooms and book out months in advance—especially in summer and fall.

**What to Bring:**
Sunscreen, torchlight, mosquito repellent, and a sense of curiosity. Some locations have no phone signal or Wi-Fi, so download maps in advance and treat it as a welcome digital detox.

Farmstays: Rustic Charm and Local Life

If you'd rather swap city lights for paddocks and animals, a farmstay can be an eye-opening way to spend a few nights. These are often family-run properties, spread across New South Wales, Victoria, and South Australia. You'll find working sheep farms, cattle stations, and hobby farms offering overnight stays with varying levels of guest involvement.

Some farmstays include optional activities: collecting eggs at dawn, feeding lambs, helping shear sheep, or watching how cheese is made. Others simply offer a warm cottage to stay in, with the countryside as your backyard. They're especially rewarding for families with young kids or travelers craving a more grounded pace.

**Average Costs:**

- Basic farm cottage: AU$100–AU$180 per night
- Farm B&B with meals and experiences: AU$200–AU$350 per night

**Meals and Inclusions:**
Many farmstays include breakfast, and some even offer dinner made from their own gardens and livestock. Don't expect hotel service—this is about hospitality in its truest form.

**Where to Book:**
Websites like **FarmStayPlanet**, **YouCamp/Hipcamp**, and even regional tourism pages list verified hosts. It's worth reading reviews to get a feel for how hands-on the experience is.

Remote Cabins and Wilderness Escapes

For travelers chasing solitude or just wanting to get away from the buzz, remote cabins are some of the most rewarding stays. Found in places like the Flinders Ranges, Western Australia's South Coast, or inland Tasmania, these cabins are often off-grid, self-catered, and far from any neighbors. What they offer in return is silence, starlight, and unfiltered access to the natural world.

Some cabins sit by rivers or lakes, others cling to cliffs or nestle in eucalyptus forests. Most have simple kitchens, outdoor fire pits, and views that feel like they were made for you alone. There's something deeply satisfying about pouring a cup of tea on a cold morning, watching mist rise from the hills, and knowing there's no schedule to keep.

**Typical Costs:**

- Budget off-grid cabin: AU$90–AU$150 per night
- Well-equipped remote cabin: AU$180–AU$350 per night
- Premium designer-style cabins: AU$400–AU$800 per night

**What to Expect:**
No room service, no crowds, often no phone signal. Some cabins require a 4WD or dirt-road driving, and many are self-check-in. Heating is often via wood fire. Insects and wildlife are part of the experience, so a flashlight and good boots come in handy.

Choosing Based on Season and Travel Style

- **Summer (December–February):** Great for coastal eco-lodges and mountain cabins. Be mindful of bushfire risks in remote areas.
- **Autumn (March–May):** Ideal for farmstays and inland cabins. The weather is mild and the crowds thinner.

- **Winter (June–August):** Perfect for alpine cabins and fireplace stays in Victoria, Tasmania, and New South Wales.
- **Spring (September–November):** Lush landscapes and wildflowers, especially in Western Australia and rural Queensland. A good season for soft hiking and wildlife spotting.

Tips for Booking and Staying

- **Plan Ahead:** Unique stays are usually limited in capacity and can be fully booked months in advance.
- **Check Accessibility:** Some locations may require private vehicles, high-clearance cars, or detailed directions to find.
- **Understand the Amenities:** Always confirm what's included—Wi-Fi, electricity, linen, and heating vary from place to place.
- **Respect the Environment:** Leave no trace, avoid loud music, and follow the recycling or composting rules if provided.

Spending a night—or several—in one of these unique Australian stays changes the rhythm of a trip. Instead of rushing from site to site, there's a moment to breathe, to watch a kangaroo hop past the cabin window, or to chat with a local farmer over a cup of tea. These aren't just beds to sleep in. They're part of the story, part of what makes the journey linger long after returning home.

## 4.3 Budget Options: Hostels, Campgrounds, and Airbnbs

Traveling across Australia doesn't have to come with a high price tag. In fact, some of the most memorable stays are found in the country's hostels, campgrounds, and budget rentals. These aren't just fallback options for shoestring travelers. They're places where connections are made, money is saved, and local life feels more accessible.

Australia has long embraced backpacker culture. With its sprawling landscape and adventure-ready cities, it's a favorite for solo travelers, gap-year wanderers, and folks who want to stretch their dollar while seeing as much as possible. Whether you're looking for a sociable hostel in Sydney, a basic beachside cabin near Byron Bay, or a cozy room in someone's Airbnb in Adelaide, there are plenty of ways to keep your accommodation costs down without sacrificing comfort or character.

Hostels: Social, Central, and Cost-Effective

Hostels in Australia range from lively backpacker spots with rooftop bars to quieter, family-friendly stays with private rooms and tidy shared kitchens. Many hostels now offer more than just dorm beds. You'll find private double rooms, female-only dorms, and even small en suite studios, especially in bigger cities.

In cities like Melbourne, Brisbane, and Perth, centrally located hostels put you right near train stations, nightlife, and food markets. Along the coast, particularly in surf towns and along the East Coast route from Sydney to Cairns, hostels become laid-back hubs for travelers sharing tips and stories over breakfast or beach bonfires.

**Cost Range (per night):**

- Dorm bed: AU$30–AU$60
- Private room: AU$85–AU$130
- En suite room: AU$120–AU$180

**Booking Tips:**
Sites like Hostelworld, Booking.com, and YHA Australia offer up-to-date listings and traveler reviews. Try to book ahead in peak seasons (summer and school holidays), especially in tourist-heavy spots like Byron Bay, Noosa, and Cairns.

**What to Expect:**
Shared bathrooms, communal kitchens, lockers, laundry facilities, and social events. Some hostels offer free breakfast, walking tours, or even surfboard rentals. Most require a key deposit and photo ID at check-in.

Campgrounds and Holiday Parks: Nature on a Budget

Camping in Australia isn't just for rugged outdoor types. The country's campgrounds and holiday parks offer a wide spectrum—from bare-bones bush camping to fully equipped sites with hot showers, swimming pools, and camp kitchens. You'll find these scattered everywhere: coastal stretches, national parks, outback towns, and even close to major cities.

**Types of Camping:**

- **Basic Campsites:** Often run by national parks or local councils. Facilities can be minimal—sometimes just pit toilets and no electricity.
- **Caravan Parks/Holiday Parks:** Great for campervans or families. Usually offer powered/unpowered sites, cabins, BBQ areas, and kids' play zones.
- **Free Camping:** Common in remote areas or roadside stops. Rules vary by state, so check local signage and apps before setting up.

**Cost Range (per night):**

- Unpowered tent site: AU$10–AU$25
- Powered campervan site: AU$25–AU$50
- Cabin in holiday park: AU$80–AU$150
- National park site: AU$10–AU$30

**Booking Resources:**

Check out **WikiCamps Australia**, **Hipcamp**, or **CamperMate** apps for listings, availability, and user reviews. Parks Australia and state national park websites also list designated campgrounds with real-time availability.

**Equipment Tips:**

If renting a car or campervan, some companies offer tents and gear as add-ons. Otherwise, budget camping stores like Kmart or Big W offer low-cost supplies. If you're only camping a few nights, buying secondhand gear from local classifieds can save money.

Airbnbs and Private Rentals: Local Living, Flexible Pricing

Airbnb is well-established in Australia, with a huge variety of listings—from shared rooms in suburban homes to entire beachfront bungalows. It's especially useful for stays in small towns where hotels or hostels are limited. If you're staying more than a couple of nights or traveling in a pair or group, Airbnb can be cheaper per person than a hotel or hostel.

In cities like Hobart, Adelaide, and Canberra, it's easy to find stylish apartments at mid-range prices. In regional areas, you'll come across quirky options like converted sheds, tiny houses, or bush cabins with outdoor baths. The platform allows you to filter by amenities, self-check-in, kitchens, laundry access, and cancellation flexibility.

**Cost Range (per night):**

- Shared room or private room: AU$40–AU$90
- Entire apartment/studio: AU$90–AU$180
- Special stays or remote options: AU$200+ (varies by season and demand)

**Tips for Booking:**

- Set a nightly budget filter and always check cleaning fees.
- Look at the location on the map—some listings say "Melbourne" but are far out in the suburbs.
- Superhosts tend to offer smoother experiences, especially for first-time travelers.
- Read reviews for noise, check-in ease, and Wi-Fi reliability.

What to Consider When Booking Budget Accommodation

1. **Location vs. Price Trade-off:**
   Staying outside city centers is often cheaper, but transportation costs can cancel out the savings. If you're relying on public transport, proximity to bus or train lines matters.

2. **Meal Options:**
   Many hostels and Airbnbs include access to a kitchen, which helps cut down food expenses. Grocery stores like Woolworths and Coles are everywhere, and most towns have local markets for fresh produce.

3. **Safety and Cleanliness:**
   Read reviews before booking. Most budget accommodations are clean and safe, but it's always good to check for past complaints.

4. **Flexibility:**
   Some hostels allow walk-ins, but many fill up quickly in peak season. Airbnb listings often offer discounts for weekly stays, and flexible cancellation policies are worth the extra few dollars.

5. **Seasonal Demand:**
   Expect higher prices during school holidays, major festivals (like Vivid Sydney or Melbourne Cup), and summer months (December–February). Booking early helps secure better rates.


Who Should Consider These Budget Stays?

- **Solo Travelers:** Hostels offer community, safety, and helpful local info.
- **Couples on a Budget:** Airbnb studios or cabins strike a nice balance between comfort and cost.
- **Families:** Holiday parks with cabins and play areas are kid-friendly and affordable.
- **Long-Term Travelers:** Monthly discounts on Airbnb and hostel work-exchange programs make it easier to extend your trip.

Budget stays don't mean cutting corners on experience. In fact, they often bring travelers closer to the ground—meeting locals, joining group hikes, or stargazing from a quiet rural campground. These accommodations can shift the entire rhythm of a trip. There's less pressure to rush and more space to breathe, listen, and take in what Australia offers when the day slows down.

Whether it's sharing stories in a hostel lounge, sipping tea on a farm cabin porch, or waking up to the scent of eucalyptus at a bush campsite, the savings go beyond money. They become part of how the journey feels—authentic, present, and rooted in real-life Australia.

## 4.4 Booking Tips and Peak Season Advice

Booking a place to stay in Australia might seem straightforward at first, but with so many options—hotels, hostels, campgrounds, eco-lodges, short-term rentals—it helps to have a game plan. Whether you're planning a city break in Sydney, a coastal escape along the Great Ocean Road, or an Outback road trip, a few well-timed decisions can save you money, stress, and disappointment.

The trick is knowing when and how to book. Australia's seasons don't always follow the typical tourist rhythms of the northern hemisphere. While December to February is peak summer here, it's also when prices rise the fastest and places sell out the quickest. On the other hand, shoulder seasons can offer better rates and more relaxed travel. By keeping a few key tips in mind, you'll be better prepared to lock in good accommodations while avoiding peak-season headaches.

Start Early, Especially for Popular Spots

Booking accommodation in advance is a smart move across most parts of Australia. In major cities, it's often possible to find a room last-minute, but in smaller towns, beach destinations, and remote regions, early booking makes all the difference—especially during peak travel months.

**When to book:**

- **Peak Season (Dec–Feb):** At least 2–4 months ahead for places like Sydney, Melbourne, Gold Coast, Byron Bay, and Cairns.
- **Shoulder Season (Mar–May, Sep–Nov):** 1–2 months ahead is usually safe.
- **Low Season (Jun–Aug):** More flexible, though popular ski areas like Thredbo or Falls Creek still require early planning.
- **Events and holidays:** For big events like New Year's Eve in Sydney or Melbourne's Grand Prix in March, bookings should be made 6 months in advance if possible.

Understand Peak Seasons by Region

Australia's peak travel seasons vary by location, so timing your booking depends a lot on where you're headed:

- **Coastal cities (Sydney, Brisbane, Perth):** Summer is peak time. Expect full bookings around Christmas and New Year.
- **Tropical North (Darwin, Cairns, Broome):** Peak season runs from May to October, when it's dry and cooler. Book early for July–August.
- **Outback regions (Alice Springs, Uluru):** Winter is high season, from June to August. Days are warm and nights are cool.
- **Snowy Mountains (NSW and VIC ski fields):** June through August is the busiest, especially July school holidays.
- **Tasmania:** Summer is the most popular season, but autumn and spring see plenty of travelers too.

Knowing this helps you spot quieter months when rates drop and availability opens up. Late spring or early autumn can be the sweet spot for both price and weather.

Compare Platforms Before You Commit

Most accommodations are listed across multiple platforms, so comparing listings helps catch better prices or perks. A few minutes of comparison shopping can save you a surprising amount.

**Popular platforms include:**

- **Booking.com:** Reliable for hotels, hostels, and apartments with lots of filter options.
- **Airbnb:** Great for private rooms, entire homes, or remote stays.
- **Expedia & Hotels.com:** Often bundled with flights for extra savings.
- **Hostelworld:** Ideal for budget travelers wanting sociable, flexible stays.
- **Agoda:** Sometimes offers lower prices, especially for last-minute deals.
- **Stayz:** Australian equivalent of Vrbo, often used for family holiday homes.
- **National Park websites (like Parks Victoria or NSW National Parks):** For campsites, cabins, and eco-friendly lodging.

Look closely at cancellation policies. Flexible bookings may cost a little more upfront but can be a lifesaver if your plans change.

Check for Seasonal Pricing and Minimum Nights

Prices across Australia fluctuate with demand. That means the same beachfront cabin in January can cost twice as much as it would in May. Some properties also apply minimum stay requirements during holiday periods, often 2 to 5 nights.

**Examples of seasonal price changes:**

- **Sydney CBD Hotel in January:** AU$250–AU$500 per night
- **Same hotel in May:** AU$150–AU$300 per night
- **Beach cabin in Noosa during Christmas week:** AU$300+ per night with 4-night minimum
- **Same cabin in September:** AU$180–AU$220 per night with no minimum stay

Planning around these shifts helps stretch your budget. Consider visiting just before or after peak dates to enjoy similar weather with fewer crowds and lower prices.

Use Travel Alerts and Price Tracking Tools

Websites and apps now make it easier to watch prices and lock in deals.

**Helpful tools:**

- **Google Travel or Kayak:** Lets you track prices and get alerts when rates drop.
- **Hopper App:** Predicts whether to book now or wait, based on price trends.
- **Skyscanner:** Includes both flights and accommodation with filters for budget and flexibility.
- **Email alerts from booking platforms:** Signing up may get you loyalty discounts or early access to sales.

Avoid Booking Mistakes Travelers Often Make

1. **Not checking the map:** A listing that says "Melbourne" might be in the far suburbs, meaning long commutes.
2. **Overlooking peak-event overlaps:** Local festivals, school breaks, or public holidays can drive prices up unexpectedly.
3. **Forgetting to read the fine print:** Cleaning fees, extra charges, or security deposits can turn a cheap stay into a pricey one.
4. **Not budgeting for transportation:** Staying outside city centers might save money on a room but cost more in daily commuting.
5. **Booking too late in remote areas:** In small towns or rural regions, choices can be limited and sell out quickly.

Be Flexible Where You Can

If you're open to changing dates, you'll often find better deals midweek or just before/after busy periods. Traveling in late February instead of early January, or choosing a Sunday–Thursday stay instead of weekends, can make a noticeable difference in price.

You might also get lower rates by staying just outside popular areas. Instead of Bondi Beach, consider Coogee. Instead of staying in the center of Byron Bay, try Suffolk Park or Lennox Head.

Save with Loyalty Programs and Direct Bookings

Some hotels and booking platforms offer rewards for returning guests. It's worth signing up for loyalty programs like:

- **Booking.com Genius**
- **Hotels.com Rewards (1 free night for every 10 booked)**
- **Accor Live Limitless (covers Mercure, Novotel, Sofitel, etc.)**
- **Qantas Hotels (earn frequent flyer points)**

Also, don't hesitate to check the property's own website. Direct bookings sometimes include perks like free breakfast, upgrades, or late checkout.

Plan Around Public Holidays and School Breaks

Australia has several public holidays that vary by state. School holidays, especially during summer, are also busy travel periods. Booking during these times often means paying more and facing stiffer competition.

**Key dates to watch:**

- **Christmas & New Year (Dec 24–Jan 2):** Peak demand nationwide
- **Australia Day (Jan 26):** Popular for domestic travel
- **Easter long weekend:** Moves each year, usually in March or April
- **School holidays:** Occur four times a year, with summer holidays in Dec–Jan being the longest

Use state-specific calendars to avoid surprises, especially if driving or visiting national parks.

Booking smart in Australia doesn't just save money—it shapes the whole rhythm of your trip. A well-located stay with flexible terms, fair pricing, and comfortable amenities can turn an ordinary visit into something relaxed and fulfilling. With some planning and a little insider awareness, the process becomes less about guesswork and more about matching your travel style with the perfect place to land.

# 5. Top Destinations and Experiences

## 5.1 Sydney: Iconic Sights and Coastal Walks

Arriving in Sydney by air is like being dropped straight into a cinematic postcard. As the plane descends over the Pacific, patches of turquoise and emerald appear between golden stretches of coastline. From above, the city feels like a mosaic of beaches, blue water, and sprawling neighborhoods—all orbiting the glittering hub of Sydney Harbour. For many travelers, this is the gateway to Australia, and its first impression rarely disappoints.

The heartbeat of Sydney can be felt at Circular Quay. Ferries chug across the harbor, their wakes trailing in soft white ribbons. Street performers juggle, dance, and sing along the promenade. The salty air is warm, but fresh, and the sunlight reflects off the rippling water in sharp flashes. This is where two of Sydney's most beloved icons meet: the Sydney Opera House and the Sydney Harbour Bridge.

The Opera House doesn't reveal its full grandeur at once. From afar, it looks like a sculpted set of sails frozen in motion. Up close, the thousands of creamy white tiles shimmer subtly, each one catching the light differently. Tourists gather on the steps to take photos, but it's the quiet corners—between the broad staircases and beneath the soaring eaves—where the building feels sacred. Guided tours inside cost around AUD 43, offering a behind-the-scenes look at its performance halls and architectural marvels.

Just across the water stands the Harbour Bridge, a hulking yet graceful piece of engineering. Locals affectionately call it "The Coathanger." For those seeking a literal high point, the BridgeClimb is unforgettable. Climbers ascend in small groups, harnessed and clipped onto safety lines. The wind grows stronger near the summit, and the views stretch all the way to the Blue Mountains on a clear day. Prices for the BridgeClimb start at about AUD 344 for a daytime climb, but the dusk and dawn climbs—more expensive—reward visitors with pink-streaked skies and glowing city lights.

From Circular Quay, it's easy to walk to the historic Rocks district. Cobblestone streets, sandstone pubs, and weekend markets create a slow-paced contrast to the glassy skyline nearby. This was where European settlement began, but today it feels like a well-loved corner of the city, layered with stories and small discoveries.

When the city heat builds, Bondi Beach offers relief. A thirty-minute bus ride from the city center, Bondi is everything it's known for: bronzed lifeguards, crashing waves, sunbathers lining the shore, and a relaxed buzz. The Bondi to Coogee coastal walk begins here—one of the most scenic walks in Australia. The path hugs the cliffs for about 6 kilometers, passing through Tamarama, Bronte, and Clovelly Beaches before ending in the calm coves of Coogee. Each bend reveals a new vista: surfers silhouetted against the sunrise, sandstone cliffs sculpted by wind, tidal pools brimming with life.

At the halfway point in Bronte, locals sip flat whites at beachfront cafes while kids play barefoot in grassy parks. The walk takes about two hours at a leisurely pace, but it's easy to lose track of time. The colors of the sea shift with the light, and the ocean breeze seems to carry the stress away. No entry fee is required, though it's worth bringing a few dollars for coffee, snacks, or a refreshing gelato.

Sydney's charm isn't confined to the coast. Darling Harbour pulses with restaurants, museums, and waterside attractions. Families wander through SEA LIFE Aquarium (tickets from AUD 39), while couples linger over dinner at harborside tables. For a different perspective, hop aboard a ferry to Manly. The 30-minute ride (AUD 10.20 one way with an Opal card) offers sweeping views of the skyline and sails. Once in Manly, travelers find a more laid-back rhythm: tree-lined promenades, small surf shops, and a beach that stretches as far as the eye can see.

One of the best ways to take in the breadth of Sydney's landscape is from the water. Harbor cruises range from basic sightseeing boats to luxury dinner cruises with multi-course meals and live music. Expect to pay anywhere from AUD 40 for a simple cruise to AUD 150+ for more elaborate experiences. Sailing past the Opera House at golden hour, glass in hand, the city feels both vast and intimate.

Inland, the Royal Botanic Garden offers a quieter, greener side of Sydney. Just steps from the Opera House, its winding paths and manicured lawns attract joggers, picnickers, and curious wanderers. The gardens are free to enter, with guided tours available for those curious about native flora and Aboriginal cultural history. From Mrs Macquarie's Chair, perched on a rocky promontory, there's a postcard-perfect view of the harbor and its landmarks—a spot that seems tailor-made for reflection.

Sydney's weather makes it a year-round destination, though the best months to visit are September through November and March through May. These shoulder seasons offer mild temperatures, fewer crowds, and more affordable accommodations. Peak summer (December to February) brings vibrant beach culture and plenty of festivals, but also higher prices and heavier tourist traffic. Budget travelers should expect to spend about AUD 150–200 per day, covering accommodation, food, transport, and entry fees to major sights. Mid-range travelers might spend AUD 250–350 per day, depending on activities and dining choices.

The city's public transport network—trains, buses, ferries, and the light rail—makes it easy to explore without a car. An Opal card is the most convenient way to pay, with daily fare caps that help keep costs down. Rides within the city center typically cost between AUD 2 and AUD 5.

What makes Sydney so unforgettable isn't just the postcard images—it's how those places feel when they're lived in. The soft breeze along the Bondi cliffs. The echo inside the Opera House foyer. The hush that falls as the ferry passes under the Harbour Bridge at dusk. Sydney doesn't just show itself. It invites. And for those willing to walk its coastal paths, climb its heights, and sail its waters, the city leaves something lasting—an impression that blends the thrill of arrival with the comfort of return.

## 5.2 Melbourne: Culture, Cafes, and Creativity

Melbourne breathes creativity. It doesn't shout, it hums, quietly confident in its identity as Australia's cultural heart. Walk through the city on any morning and the rhythm becomes clear: baristas steaming milk behind café counters, artists arranging canvases in street-facing galleries, students rushing toward the State Library with books tucked under their arms, and cyclists weaving through laneways painted with vibrant murals that seem to change overnight.

This city thrives in the details. In the scent of roasted beans from a coffee shop hidden behind a graffiti-covered alley. In the worn steps of Flinders Street Station, where commuters cross paths under the station clock, some headed to the suburbs, others stopping to take in the view of the Yarra River as rowers cut through its waters below. Culture lives here, not just in museums but in the everyday. It pulses through the tramlines, glows from late-night theater lights, and lingers in the air after a live gig in a Brunswick bar.

At the core of Melbourne's appeal is its layered atmosphere. Every neighborhood feels like its own city. Fitzroy bursts with bohemian charm—vintage stores, tattoo studios, and vegan eateries line the streets. Carlton whispers history through the corridors of the University of Melbourne and the Italian eateries on Lygon Street, where pasta is handmade and espresso is served short, strong, and without fuss. In Southbank, sleek high-rises mirror the flow of the river while rooftop bars serve cocktails with panoramic views that stretch to the Dandenong Ranges.

Queen Victoria Market is a must. Not only for its produce and food stalls, but for the energy that hums between vendors and shoppers. There's laughter over fishmongers' counters, the sharp clang of knives slicing fresh fruit, and the smoky scent of sizzling bratwurst. Down the tramline, the Royal Botanic Gardens offer a complete shift in pace. The city slips away, replaced by winding paths, tranquil lakes, and sun-dappled lawns where locals sprawl with books or picnic spreads.

Art and design aren't confined to galleries here, but for those who seek them, the National Gallery of Victoria (NGV) holds masterpieces behind its iconic water wall, while the Ian Potter Centre dives deep into Australian art. For a more underground feel, Hosier Lane becomes a rotating exhibition, where street artists claim their canvas, layering political commentary with bursts of color. Meanwhile, on any given evening, a tucked-away jazz bar in Collingwood might host a band that will be headlining a festival next year.

Melbourne rewards the curious. A traveler willing to step off the main roads finds secondhand bookstores stacked to the ceiling, cinema lounges screening indie films, and art collectives that double as cafés and poetry venues. Laneway discoveries often become highlights: a hidden cocktail bar down a dim stairwell, a record shop with live DJs, or a tiny eatery serving Korean-Mexican fusion tacos to a line of eager locals.

Reaching Melbourne is straightforward. International flights arrive at Melbourne Airport (Tullamarine), just 20 kilometers northwest of the city center. SkyBus shuttles provide regular service into town for around AUD 20. For those arriving from elsewhere in Australia, domestic flights connect regularly from Sydney, Brisbane, Perth, and Adelaide, while train services through Southern Cross Station link Victoria's regional hubs. Once in the city, trams are a defining part of the experience. The free City Circle tram loops through central districts, while Myki cards offer access to an extensive public network across trains, trams, and buses.

Melbourne's seasons are distinct. Summers (December to February) bring dry heat and a flood of outdoor festivals. Winter (June to August) chills the city, but it glows with fireside dining, winter markets, and arts festivals like Melbourne International Film Festival. Autumn and spring are ideal for wandering, with mild weather, golden foliage, and cultural events blooming across the calendar. Major happenings include White Night, Moomba Festival, and the Melbourne Writers Festival.

Costs vary, but travelers can expect to spend around AUD 100 to AUD 250 per night on mid-range accommodation. Budget stays dip closer to AUD 60, while boutique hotels and luxury options soar past AUD 300. Café culture thrives in Melbourne, and a flat white generally runs between AUD 4.50 to AUD 6. Brunch at a trendy café may cost around AUD 25 to AUD 35 per person, while dinner at a mid-range restaurant averages AUD 40 to AUD 70. Gallery admission is often free, though special exhibitions may charge around AUD 15 to AUD 30. Guided street art tours or culinary experiences usually start at AUD 60 and rise depending on length and inclusions.

No matter the season or budget, Melbourne finds a way into travelers' memories through its mood. It doesn't aim to impress with flash. Instead, it unfolds in layers—the kind that linger long after the last tram ride, the final espresso, the closing notes of a laneway musician. It is a city best experienced slowly, with open eyes and a curious spirit, ready to follow the next painted wall or scent of baked bread into a moment that feels entirely unique.

## 5.3 Great Barrier Reef and Tropical North Queensland

The sky above Cairns glows in soft pastels as the day begins, casting gold across the Coral Sea. From this tropical hub in Far North Queensland, adventure stretches outward in every direction—north into the Daintree Rainforest, west into the savannah, and most famously, east to the living, breathing marvel that is the Great Barrier Reef.

Spanning more than 2,300 kilometers, the reef is not one destination but a world of its own. It begins just offshore and trails all the way down the Queensland coast, visible even from space. Underneath the water's surface, a riot of life sways in slow motion—corals that bloom like underwater cities, sea turtles gliding with age-old grace, schools of neon fish darting between anemones. Few places on Earth stir such awe and humility in the same breath.

For many travelers, the first encounter with the reef begins in Cairns or Port Douglas, where catamarans and dive boats head out daily to the outer reef. The boat ride itself can be exhilarating, wind on the face and salt in the air, with the anticipation building as the water shifts from aquamarine to deep sapphire. Then comes the mask, the snorkel, the first tentative dip—and suddenly, silence. Color. Wonder.

Floating over coral gardens, the body moves almost without effort. A green sea turtle flaps by, seemingly unbothered by the human presence. Clownfish peek out from bright orange anemones, playful and watchful all at once. Deeper down, reef sharks patrol their domain with quiet authority. Time slows in the water. Everything feels bigger and smaller at once.

For those ready to go beyond snorkeling, scuba diving offers an entirely different level of immersion. Liveaboard trips allow divers to sleep under the stars on the ocean, waking up for sunrise dives when the reef comes alive in a way few ever witness. Night dives reveal glowing corals and curious reef creatures that rarely appear during daylight. There's even the option to try introductory dives for beginners—no certification needed, just a willingness to trust and breathe.

But Tropical North Queensland isn't just about the reef. Inland, the rainforest calls with a different kind of wild magic. The Daintree is the oldest tropical rainforest on Earth, a tangle of ferns, vines, and towering trees teeming with biodiversity. A short drive from Port Douglas brings travelers into Mossman Gorge, where cool, clear waters flow between smooth granite boulders. Guided walks with Indigenous Kuku Yalanji elders offer more than nature—they provide cultural depth, storytelling, and connection to the country.

Further north, Cape Tribulation lives up to its name as a place where the road narrows, the forest thickens, and mobile reception fades. It's a region that encourages letting go—of schedules, of speed, of signal. The beach here is empty and endless, where the rainforest meets the sea without interruption.

Back in Cairns or Palm Cove, the pace slows. Beachfront promenades host cafes and seafood restaurants where mud crab and fresh barramundi are staples. In the evenings, local markets buzz with color, aroma, and crafts, blending Indigenous designs with tropical flair. Palm trees sway in the warm air, and the scent of frangipani carries on the breeze.

Getting to the Great Barrier Reef region is easy, but what lies beyond is anything but simple. Direct flights arrive in Cairns from major Australian cities like Sydney, Melbourne, and Brisbane, with connections from Asia and the Pacific as well. The Cairns Airport sits just 10 minutes from the city center. Port Douglas, quieter and more upscale, is about a 1-hour drive north along one of the most scenic coastal roads in the country.

Most reef tours depart from Cairns or Port Douglas, with full-day snorkeling trips averaging AUD 180 to 250 per person. Introductory scuba dives usually start around AUD 300, while multi-day liveaboard diving expeditions can range from AUD 800 to over AUD 2,000 depending on duration and season. National park access fees are often included in these tours, but it's worth checking in advance.

For land-based exploring, Daintree guided tours typically cost around AUD 180 to 220 for full-day experiences, often with river cruises to spot crocodiles or rainforest hikes. Renting a car is the best way to experience the region beyond the reef, with daily rates starting at AUD 60 for economy options.

The best time to visit the reef and the tropical north is during the dry season—from May to October—when temperatures range between 20°C to 29°C, and humidity is low. This period avoids the tropical summer's heavy rains and stinger season, although stinger suits are provided on tours year-round as a precaution.

Accommodations run the full spectrum—from budget hostels at AUD 35 per night to high-end eco-resorts in the Daintree at over AUD 400 per night. Palm Cove offers boutique beachside stays with spa packages and sea views, while Cairns caters to every traveler with motels, mid-range hotels, and family-friendly apartments.

But more than prices or logistics, what matters here is the feeling. The feeling of lying on the deck of a boat at dusk, watching the sky catch fire behind the Coral Sea. The feeling of sand between toes after a forest walk. The sound of cicadas at night. The hushed joy of seeing a breaching humpback whale in the distance or spotting a cassowary across a jungle road like it owns the place—because it does.

Tropical North Queensland doesn't just check off boxes. It resets something in the spirit. It invites stillness, wonder, and respect for the balance of reef, rainforest, and people. In the end, those who come for the reef often leave remembering the silence of the water, the warmth of the sun, and the stories that linger long after the trip ends.

## 5.4 Red Centre: Uluru, Alice Springs, and Outback Adventures

Red dirt stretches endlessly in every direction. The air carries the dry scent of eucalyptus and iron-rich soil. Overhead, the sky feels impossibly big—clearer, bluer, more open than anywhere else. This is the heart of Australia, the Red Centre, where vastness meets stillness, and the land speaks in silence.

At its core rises Uluru, the massive sandstone monolith that has stood watch for millions of years. More than a landmark, it's a presence. From a distance, it appears burnt orange and unmoving. But as the sun shifts, Uluru changes—glowing crimson at sunset, washed with lavender before dawn. It's alive in the way ancient things are, holding stories within its deep grooves and caves. The local Anangu people, Traditional Owners of the land, call it Tjukurpa—a word that carries law, culture, and creation in one breath.

Standing at the base of Uluru, surrounded by the soft crunch of desert sand, everything quiets. Guided walks around the rock—particularly the Mala and Kuniya walks—reveal sacred sites, cave paintings, and the stories tied to the rock's formation. Anangu rangers share legends passed down for generations. These aren't just tales—they're teachings, connected to the land, the sky, and the creatures that still move through this arid world.

Nearby, Kata Tjuta (the Olgas) rises in a cluster of rounded domes, taller even than Uluru. The Valley of the Winds walk leads through narrow gorges and sweeping plateaus, where desert winds whisper and wedge-tailed eagles circle high above. The heat here can be fierce, especially in summer, but the beauty cuts through it. Few places evoke such reverence.

About 450 kilometers northeast lies Alice Springs, a town shaped by resilience, creativity, and contrast. It's both remote and alive with a community, surrounded by ancient ranges and desert flora. Art galleries here showcase Aboriginal works unlike anywhere else in the country—bold dot paintings, earthy colors, and stories tied to Dreamtime mythology.

The Alice Springs Desert Park provides a powerful introduction to the ecosystems of the Outback. Kangaroos, emus, and thorny devils live among spinifex and mulga trees. Night tours reveal shy nocturnal creatures—bilbies, echidnas, and ghost bats. Every species here has adapted not just to survive, but to thrive in extremes.

Adventure in the Red Centre often means dust, stars, and the open road. The Red Centre Way is a loop that connects Alice Springs, Kings Canyon, Watarrka National Park, and Uluru-Kata Tjuta National Park. Along the way, ancient gorges cut through rock layers older than most continents. Kings Canyon offers some of the region's most dramatic scenery—cliffs that plunge into fern-lined crevices, domes that look like beehives from the sky. The Rim Walk, especially at sunrise, is both a physical and spiritual journey.

Driving the Red Centre is a rite of passage. Roads stretch straight to the horizon, flanked by spinifex plains and ghost gum trees. Roadhouses break up the silence with petrol, meat pies, and friendly banter. It's not about speed but presence—slowing down enough to notice how the desert changes hour by hour.

Getting here requires a bit more effort than coastal destinations, but that's part of its appeal. Daily flights connect Alice Springs and Ayers Rock Airport (Yulara) to major cities like Sydney, Melbourne, and Darwin. From Alice Springs, it's about a 4.5 to 5-hour drive to Uluru, mostly along sealed roads. A 3-day 4WD rental typically starts at AUD 400–600 depending on vehicle and season. Alternatively, guided tours depart from Alice Springs and include transport, meals, camping gear, and cultural talks—ranging from AUD 800 to AUD 1,200 for a 3-day itinerary.

Park passes for Uluru-Kata Tjuta cost AUD 38 per adult (valid for 3 days), and sunrise or sunset tours often cost around AUD 70–150. For a once-in-a-lifetime experience, the "Field of Light" art installation by Bruce Munro spreads over the desert near Uluru, glowing with 50,000 solar-powered stems after dark—entry starts at AUD 44.

Accommodations vary widely. Yulara, the resort township near Uluru, offers everything from five-star stays like Sails in the Desert (starting at AUD 400 per night) to budget lodges and campgrounds (from AUD 40 per night). Alice Springs has a mix of motels, hostels, and cozy guesthouses. Remote eco-lodges near Kings Canyon provide unforgettable views under a sky flooded with stars.

The best time to visit the Red Centre is during the cooler months—from April to September—when daytime temperatures range from 18°C to 28°C and nights are crisp. Summer (December to February) can bring scorching heat over 40°C and is best avoided for hiking unless properly prepared.

What makes this region unforgettable isn't just the scenery—it's the feeling. Watching the sun rise over Uluru is quiet and humbling. Sitting around a campfire with red dust on boots and a billion stars overhead feels timeless. Listening to stories from an Anangu guide, seeing ancient symbols painted on rock, or spotting a dingo trotting across the road—all leave an imprint.

The Outback strips things down to what matters. It teaches patience, presence, and respect. It invites visitors to be still, to listen, and to see not just with their eyes, but with something deeper.

## 5.5 Tasmania: Wilderness and Wildlife

The ferry edges away from Melbourne, slicing across the Bass Strait. Hours later, Tasmania appears like a whisper on the horizon—rugged, green, and misted in clouds. For those who make the journey, it often feels like stepping into another rhythm. Life slows. Silence returns. The wilderness takes over.

Tasmania, Australia's island state, isn't loud. It doesn't shout for attention. Instead, it draws people in with quiet force: wild coasts where waves pound against sea cliffs, ancient rainforests wrapped in mist, and highland lakes so still they reflect the sky like mirrors. It's where nature leads the story.

Cradle Mountain is often the first name to surface when travelers think of Tasmania. It doesn't disappoint. The jagged dolerite peak, often dusted in snow even as valleys bloom with wildflowers, rises beside Dove Lake like a painting come to life. Walking the six-kilometer Dove Lake Circuit, boardwalks wind through button grass, twisted snow gums, and mirrored water. Wombats shuffle through the undergrowth. Wallabies twitch in the shadows. The air smells of cold stone and wet moss.

For those who venture further, the Overland Track is Tasmania's legendary multi-day trek—a 65-kilometer journey through alpine meadows, forests, waterfalls, and remote highlands. It's a test of endurance and wonder, best tackled between October and May when weather allows. Huts along the way offer shelter, but the wild remains constant. Permits cost around AUD 200 in peak season, and while it's possible to go self-guided, many choose small-group tours for support and storytelling along the way.

Tasmania is built for explorers. In the southwest, the wilderness becomes truly remote. Southwest National Park, part of the larger Tasmanian Wilderness World Heritage Area, covers over 600,000 hectares of untouched terrain. There are no roads into its heart—only light aircraft, long hikes, or boat access. Melaleuca, a tiny outpost, acts as a portal into this lost world. Few travelers come here, but those who do speak of rivers so clear they reveal fish gliding over quartzite stones, and forests that haven't changed in millennia.

Along the east coast, the mood softens. Freycinet National Park feels more Mediterranean than sub-Antarctic.

Tasmania's wildlife is not confined to parks—it's part of the everyday. At dusk near Narawntapu National Park on the north coast, dozens of wallabies and Forester kangaroos graze on grassy plains. In the forests near Mount Field, glow worms flicker along mossy banks. And on Bruny Island, fairy penguins waddle ashore in twilight, returning from the sea in groups, heads tilted curiously at the small crowds watching from designated hides.

But perhaps no animal is as iconic—or misunderstood—as the Tasmanian devil. At Bonorong Wildlife Sanctuary just outside Hobart, visitors can see these feisty, nocturnal marsupials up close. Much smaller than cartoons would suggest, they're also louder, their growls echoing in the night. The sanctuary plays a vital role in conservation, especially with devils suffering from a contagious facial tumor disease in the wild. Entry is around AUD 36 for adults, and guided tours provide intimate insights into the island's creatures.

Hobart, the capital, is a natural base. It blends colonial charm with natural beauty. Mount Wellington looms behind the city—snow-capped in winter, windswept and wild year-round. The summit, accessible by car or bike, offers views stretching from the Derwent River to distant peaks. Below, Salamanca Place comes alive each Saturday with market stalls, handmade crafts, fresh produce, and street musicians echoing off sandstone walls. The cost of a city stay is modest compared to mainland capitals—expect mid-range hotels to range from AUD 130 to AUD 220 per night, with boutique and historic inns often slightly higher.

Ferries to Bruny Island cost under AUD 50 return (per vehicle) and make for an easy day or overnight trip. Bushwalks, beaches, and wildlife experiences define the island. For coastal adventurers, guided boat tours around Bruny's sea cliffs offer a chance to see fur seals, migrating whales (in season), and rare sea birds. Expect prices around AUD 135 for a half-day cruise.

For travelers chasing peace, Maria Island is unmatched. No cars, no shops, no Wi-Fi. Just barefoot trails, empty beaches, and wildlife everywhere—wombats graze near abandoned cottages, Cape Barren geese march through the grasslands, and the Painted Cliffs ripple with ancient marine life. The ferry from Triabunna takes under 30 minutes and costs AUD 50 return. Camping is popular, though basic bunkhouses are available for those wanting a roof.

Tasmania's climate adds to its mystique. Summers (December to February) are warm and dry, ideal for coastal hikes and kayaking, with daytime highs between 20°C and 25°C. Autumn brings color to the highlands, especially around Lake St Clair and the Central Plateau. Winter is crisp and moody, with snow dusting the mountains—perfect for fireside cabins and photography. Spring bursts with wildflowers and baby animals. Layers are essential; weather can change quickly, especially at higher elevations.

Getting to Tasmania is simpler than many expect. Regular flights connect Hobart and Launceston to Melbourne (1 hour), Sydney (1 hour 45 minutes), and Brisbane (2.5 hours), with round-trip fares often starting at AUD 180–300 depending on season. The Spirit of Tasmania ferry departs daily from Geelong and takes about 9–11 hours overnight, with prices starting around AUD 99 for walk-on passengers and AUD 240+ for vehicles.

Tasmania rewards curiosity. It doesn't rush. It waits—for hikers to reach the summit, for devils to emerge from burrows, for clouds to part over a mirror-still lake. Travelers come here for wilderness, but what they often find is clarity: in the air, in the silence, in themselves.

There's a calm in Tasmania that's hard to explain but easy to feel. A sense that nature is not something to be conquered, but to be understood and respected. For those willing to go beyond the mainland, it's not just a destination—it's a state of mind.

## 5.6 Western Australia: Perth, Coral Coast, and Remote Beauty

Western Australia doesn't reveal itself quickly. It asks for time. For distance. For a willingness to look past the tourist trails and follow the long roads that stretch into red earth and blinding blue. But for those who do, what unfolds is unforgettable—sun-drenched beaches without crowds, landscapes layered with age and color, and a city that balances isolation with surprising sophistication.

At the edge of the continent lies Perth. Vastly removed from Australia's eastern capitals, Perth pulses to its own rhythm. The Indian Ocean gleams to the west, and golden light pours over the Swan River each afternoon. Kings Park, one of the largest inner-city parks in the world, rises above the skyline with its native bushland, war memorials, and panoramic lookouts. Locals jog past wildflowers and picnickers, and when the breeze carries scents of eucalyptus, the city feels like it's holding its breath.

The beaches here don't compete for attention. They don't need to. Cottesloe's curve of white sand, backed by Norfolk pines and café patios, is where locals gather for sunset swims and fish and chips on the grass. Scarborough offers something wilder—surfers carving lines through turquoise water and beach volleyball courts buzzing with energy. And then there's City Beach, quieter, expansive, where the sand feels like sifted flour underfoot and the ocean's edge stretches far beyond sight.

Drive just 30 minutes from central Perth, and the Swan Valley emerges: a region of orchards, bush trails, and working farms. While often overshadowed by the more famous Margaret River further south, the Swan Valley offers a relaxed, close-to-city retreat. It's a good place to try local honey, handmade nougat, and artisan cheeses—all with kangaroos sometimes grazing nearby in the golden light of evening.

A few hours' drive south, the coastline begins to ripple and twist. The Margaret River region, is just as defined by towering karri forests and caves laced beneath the surface. Travelers can explore Jewel Cave or Mammoth Cave, where stalactites hang like chandeliers and underground rivers echo the pulse of ancient time. Along the coast, the Indian Ocean smashes against limestone at Cape Leeuwin, where two oceans—the Indian and the Southern  visibly meet.

But to really grasp Western Australia's grandeur, go north. Here, the journey becomes part of the experience.

The Coral Coast stretches for over 1,000 kilometers between Perth and Exmouth, hugging a shoreline of deep blues and ochres. Along the way lies Kalbarri National Park, where the Murchison River cuts through red rock gorges in deep loops and curves. Nature's Window—a wind-sculpted rock arch—frames the ancient landscape like a painting. Hiking trails here are raw and rewarding, especially in the wildflower season (August to October) when the arid land bursts with color.

Further up is Shark Bay, a UNESCO World Heritage site of calm bays, ancient stromatolites, and marine life in abundance. Monkey Mia is one of its most famous pockets—known for the wild dolphins that have visited its shores for generations. Arrive early, when the rangers lead a quiet and respectful viewing as the dolphins glide into the shallows, seemingly recognizing the human ritual.

Then there's Coral Bay and Exmouth, gateways to the Ningaloo Reef. Less crowded than the Great Barrier Reef, Ningaloo is where the reef meets the beach—literally. Walk straight from shore into a world of color and life. Snorkel among coral gardens just meters from land. In the right season (March to July), it's possible to swim with whale sharks—the gentle giants of the sea. Tours leave from Exmouth or Coral Bay, starting around AUD 400, including guides and gear.

Cape Range National Park lies beside the reef, its dry canyons and rocky gorges contrasting the marine world below. Hike Mandu Mandu Gorge in the cool morning air. Watch black-footed rock wallabies dart across stone ledges. Then head down to Turquoise Bay, where currents carry snorkelers across vivid coral beds in a natural drift—a silent, surreal ride through another world.

Getting around Western Australia requires planning. Domestic flights from major cities to Perth are frequent: from Sydney or Melbourne, expect 4–5 hours in the air with round-trip fares ranging from AUD 250–500 depending on season. Renting a car or campervan is the best way to explore the wider region, especially the Coral Coast. Fuel costs vary, but in remote areas expect to pay around AUD 2.30 per liter.

Accommodations along the coast range from beach chalets and family-run motels (AUD 120–180 per night) to remote wilderness lodges or glamping stays closer to AUD 300+.

Back in Perth, Fremantle—often just called "Freo"—is where the creative soul of the city lives. This portside town feels like its own entity. Historic warehouses have become markets, cafés, art galleries, and microbreweries. The Fremantle Markets buzz with handmade goods, Indigenous art, and street food. Walk along the harbor past old convict buildings, listen to buskers echoing blues and indie folk, and stay to watch the orange sky melt into the sea.

Western Australia is vast. It's not designed for quick visits or fast lists. It asks travelers to slow down, stretch their sense of distance, and sit with the silence of space. Whether it's the far-off Kimberley region with its ancient rock formations and Aboriginal rock art, or the soft sands of Esperance in the south with kangaroos lounging on the beach, this side of Australia is built for those who crave the uncommon.

Here, the road doesn't just lead to places—it leads to a feeling. One of being small in the best possible way. Of standing at the edge of cliffs that haven't changed in millions of years. Of hearing only the wind and waves for miles. And in that quiet, Western Australia speaks.

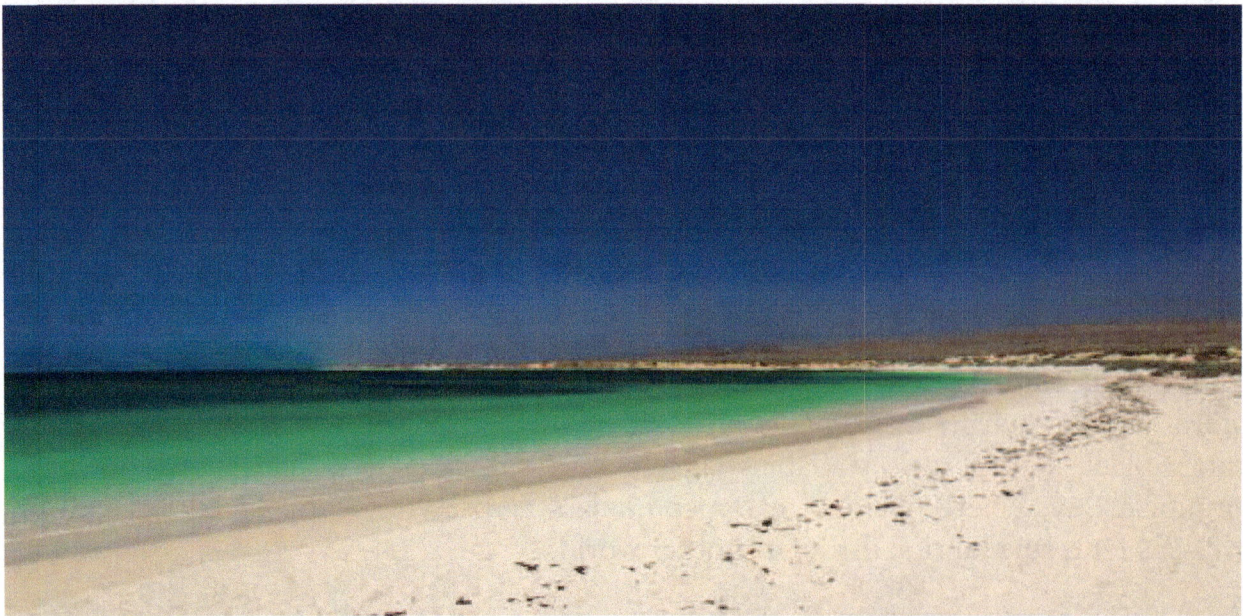

## 5.7 Wildlife Encounters and Natural Wonders

Australia feels alive in ways that few other places do. Not just because of its vast open spaces or ancient landscapes, but because so much of it moves, breathes, and watches back. Wallabies thump through dusk in the Outback. Sulphur-crested cockatoos shriek overhead in city parks. Saltwater crocodiles lounge like prehistoric kings in the Northern Territory, unmoved by the human presence watching from a safe distance. Here, nature doesn't wait to be sought—it meets travelers at every turn.

Start on Kangaroo Island, off the southern coast of Australia, where wildlife thrives in a protected paradise. This is one of the country's best spots to see animals in their natural habitat. Think of wild kangaroos bounding through eucalyptus forest, echidnas waddling along dirt tracks, and koalas curled in tree forks. At Seal Bay, a colony of sea lions basks on the sand, undisturbed by the wind or the watching eyes of respectful visitors. Guided boardwalk tours lead down to the beach, where travelers can get up close without interfering—about AUD 39 for adults, with discounts for children and families.

In the north, Kakadu National Park in the Northern Territory is another kind of marvel. It's not just vast—it's a living mosaic of wetland, rock, and escarpment that pulses with life. Crocodiles glide through billabongs with prehistoric grace. Brolgas dance in the floodplains during the monsoon. At dusk, the air comes alive with the calls of magpie geese, rainbow bee-eaters, and hundreds of other species. Boat cruises on the Yellow Water Billabong are a must—especially at sunrise or sunset. Expect to pay around AUD 100 for a 90-minute guided trip through one of Australia's richest wildlife corridors.

For those drawn to marine life, the Great Barrier Reef delivers in ways few places can. Beyond the coral and color lies a constant parade of life. Green sea turtles drift past coral gardens. Clownfish dart through anemones. From November to March, manta rays soar beneath the surface near Lady Elliot Island. In June and July, dwarf minke whales migrate through the outer reef, allowing rare snorkel encounters. Tours to swim with these whales leave from Cairns or Port Douglas, starting from around AUD 500 per person—pricey, yes, but intimate and unforgettable.

Not far from the reef, Daintree Rainforest offers another kind of encounter. This is the oldest living rainforest in the world—home to cassowaries with electric-blue necks, tree kangaroos, and green-eyed frogs. Walk along the Marrdja Boardwalk or the Jindalba circuit, where ancient ferns lean into the path and the air feels thick with chlorophyll. Guides with deep knowledge of Indigenous culture and rainforest ecosystems make the experience richer. Night walks in the forest reveal a different cast: bioluminescent fungi, sleeping birds, and the eerie eyeshine of sugar gliders.

On the western side of the continent, Ningaloo Reef offers something the Great Barrier can't—accessibility. Here, wildlife encounters begin at the shore. Reef sharks and stingrays glide through shallows, while snorkelers wade into coral gardens just meters from the beach. Whale shark season (March to July) draws thousands to Exmouth and Coral Bay. Despite their name, these creatures are gentle filter feeders, allowing swimmers to float calmly alongside. Tour costs hover around AUD 400–500, but include marine biologists, equipment, and often a videographer to capture the moment.

Back on land, the deserts of Central Australia may seem quiet, but listen closely and life emerges. Dingoes call across the night. Thorny devils—tiny lizard oddities—shuffle across the sand in search of ants. Near Uluru, the sunrise often comes with a surprise: a red kangaroo standing still against the skyline, watching before bounding off into the bush. Guided walks with local Anangu guides introduce travelers not just to animals, but to the Dreamtime stories that connect them to the land.

Tasmania, too, is a haven for wildlife. In the rugged wilderness of Cradle Mountain–Lake St Clair National Park, wombats waddle across open meadows, unconcerned by the passing of hikers. Devils @ Cradle, a conservation sanctuary, offers nighttime tours to witness Tasmanian devils feeding, growling, and interacting—a glimpse into one of Australia's most endangered and misunderstood species. The entry fee for guided evening tours is around AUD 35–45, and supports local conservation.

Even in urban areas, Australia's wildlife never feels far. In Sydney, possums peek from branches in Centennial Park, and giant fruit bats flap over Botanic Gardens at dusk. In Melbourne, the Yarra River attracts ducks, swans, and water dragons that lounge in the sun. On Phillip Island, just under two hours from Melbourne, visitors gather nightly to witness the famous Penguin Parade—hundreds of little penguins waddling up the beach to their burrows after a day at sea. General admission starts at AUD 30, with upgraded viewing platforms available for a closer look.

Birdwatchers find paradise in the wetlands of Kakadu, the coastlines of Broome, or the temperate forests of Victoria's Otway Ranges. Australia is home to more than 800 bird species, many of them endemic. The laugh of the kookaburra, the whipcrack call of the eastern whipbird, and the fluting notes of the magpie become part of the soundscape for anyone paying attention.

What makes these encounters so powerful isn't just the range of species—it's how unfiltered the experiences often feel. There are places in Australia where it's still possible to feel like a guest in someone else's world. Where the animals aren't put on display—they just live, and if you're lucky and patient, you might witness something remarkable.

Whether it's the sharp-eyed stare of a crocodile, the shy blink of a wallaby at dawn, or the slow-motion arc of a whale breaching off the southern coast, Australia's wildlife encounters connect travelers to something elemental. They remind you that despite the roads and the cities and the schedules, there's a deeper rhythm here—an older one—and it's still running strong.

# 6. Food, Drink, and Dining in Australia

## 6.1 What to Eat and Where to Find It

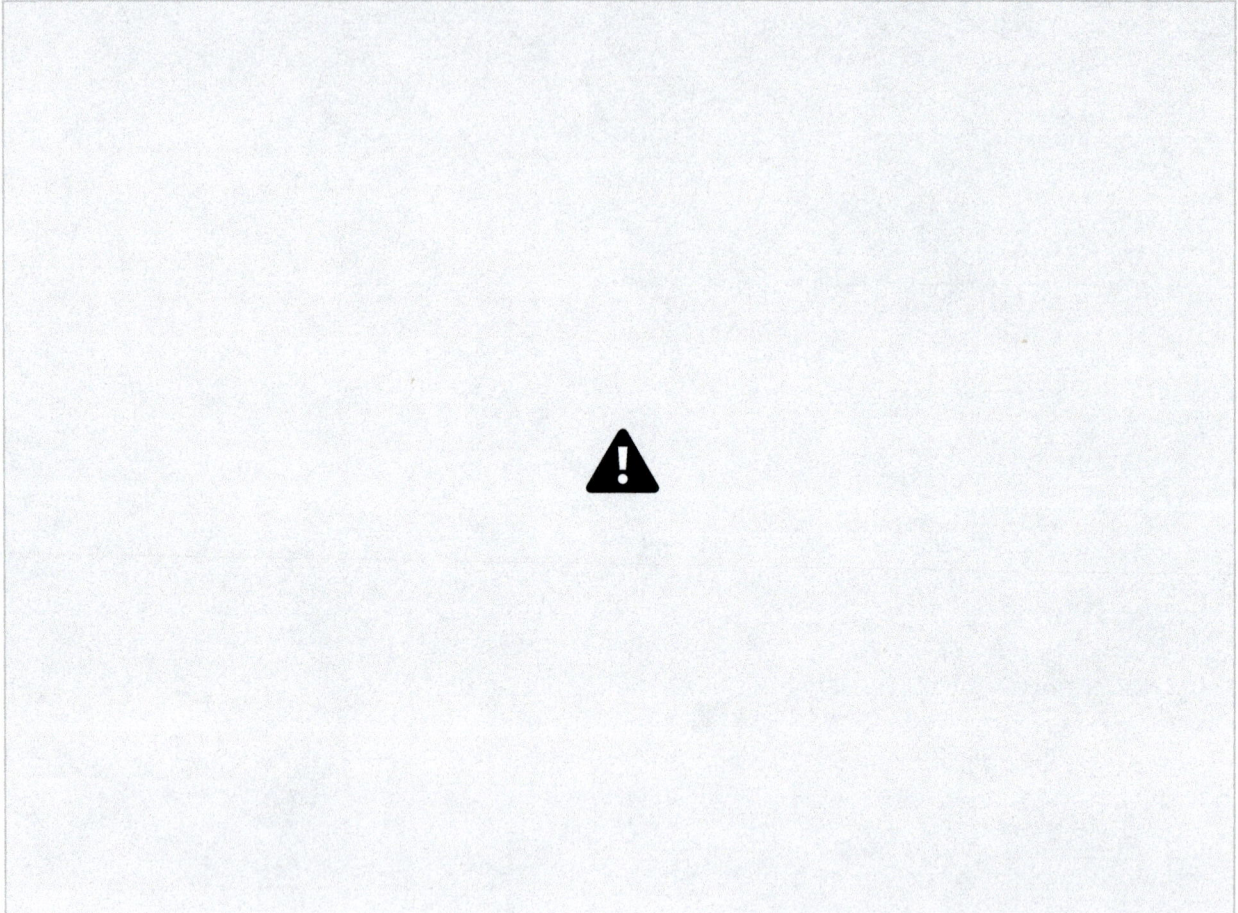

Food in Australia doesn't just reflect what's available locally—it mirrors the culture itself. It's casual, multicultural, creative, and built on a strong connection to the land and sea. Whether you're standing barefoot by a seaside fish-and-chip shop, tucking into a fragrant curry laksa in a suburban food court, or sitting under string lights in a Melbourne laneway café with sourdough toast and a perfectly poached egg, you're getting a taste of something more than just ingredients. You're getting a taste of how Australia eats: informally, globally, and often outdoors.

You might start your day with breakfast, but here, it's almost always called *brunch*, and it's a serious affair. Melbourne is the spiritual home of Australian brunch culture, where cafés serve plates that look like they were styled for a magazine shoot. Think smashed avocado on artisanal bread, shakshuka with farm eggs, and beetroot hummus smeared under heirloom tomatoes. You'll find baristas who've trained in latte art as if it's a competitive sport. A flat white is the standard coffee order, and cafés will often let you swap in oat, almond, or soy milk without blinking. Expect to pay AUD 18–24 for a brunch plate and AUD 4–6 for coffee.

Lunch might be a meat pie grabbed from a corner bakery—a handheld favorite filled with minced beef and gravy, sometimes with mushy peas on top. Or maybe it's a burger with "the lot" (beetroot, pineapple, egg, and bacon stacked inside). If you're vegetarian or gluten-free, most places will accommodate you. Vegan eateries are growing fast, especially in Sydney, Byron Bay, and Fremantle.

For dinner, the options open wide. Australia's cities are incredibly multicultural, and that shows in the food. You can find handmade Afghan dumplings in Melbourne's Dandenong Market, Sri Lankan hopper stalls in Darwin, Vietnamese banh mi in western Sydney, and fragrant Ethiopian injera platters in Adelaide. Neighborhoods often reflect immigrant communities, so it pays to ask locals where to go. Sydney's Cabramatta is known for authentic Vietnamese dishes, while Melbourne's Footscray bursts with East African and Southeast Asian flavors.

Fresh seafood is a big part of coastal life, and it's worth seeking out. Try Sydney rock oysters straight from the shell at the Sydney Fish Market, or grilled barramundi at a no-frills beachside shack in Queensland. In Tasmania, you'll spot abalone and crayfish on high-end menus. One of the simplest, most satisfying seafood meals is still fish and chips eaten straight from the paper, feet dangling off a pier.

If you're feeling adventurous, keep an eye out for dishes made with native bush foods, often called *bush tucker*. These include wattleseed, finger lime, Davidson's plum, and kangaroo or emu meat. Many Indigenous-owned cafés and restaurants now spotlight traditional ingredients in modern dishes—like crocodile spring rolls or lemon myrtle cheesecake. In the Red Centre, spots like the Mbantua Café in Alice Springs offer guided tastings with context and history.

Pub culture plays a big role in the Australian dining experience too. You'll likely end up in one at some point—either for a cheap "parma and pint" night (chicken parmigiana ), steak specials, or Sunday roasts. Most pubs have a counter where you order, grab a buzzer, and wait for your food to arrive. Don't be surprised if there's a salad bar off to the side, or if kids are running around barefoot. It's laid-back, social, and great for budget-friendly meals. Prices for pub mains hover between AUD 20 and 30.

You'll also come across a few customs worth knowing. "BYO" stands for Bring Your Own, and it's common at many small restaurants, particularly in suburban areas and regional towns.

Street food and night markets are also growing in popularity. Sydney's Chinatown Night Market (Friday nights) serves bao buns, skewers, and sizzling noodle plates under neon lights. In Darwin, the Mindil Beach Sunset Market is famous for its multicultural eats, from laksa to kangaroo satay. These are casual, lively places to eat affordably, often with live music and a view.

If you're traveling on a budget, supermarkets like Coles and Woolworths are good spots to stock up on snacks and groceries. Ready-made salads, sushi packs, and rotisserie chickens are widely available, as are meal kits. For longer stays or campervan trips, having access to a local grocery store can cut food costs dramatically. A simple grocery haul for two people for a week can range between AUD 80–150 depending on how you eat.

Vegetarians and vegans will find that Australia's food scene has come a long way. Cities like Brisbane and Hobart have growing plant-based communities, and most menus will clearly mark vegetarian or vegan options. Gluten-free eaters are also well accommodated, thanks in part to Australia's high rate of gluten intolerance.

For sweet tooths, dessert is no afterthought. Try lamingtons (sponge cake rolled in chocolate and coconut), Anzac biscuits (oat-based cookies with historical significance), and pavlova (a meringue-based dessert claimed by both Aussies and Kiwis). In summer, frozen treats like mango Weis Bars and Golden Gaytimes are nostalgic favorites available in every corner store.

Finally, there's coffee. Australian café culture isn't just a trend—it's a way of life. You'll find espresso machines in gas stations, bakeries, and outposts hundreds of kilometers from the nearest city. A *flat white* is the standard order: espresso with microfoam milk, stronger than a latte and less milky than a cappuccino. Don't expect bottomless drip coffee or flavored syrups—it's all about well-roasted beans and quality technique. Most Australians will have strong opinions about where to get the best brew, so ask around.

Every region brings its own flavors, and eating your way through the country is one of the best ways to understand how Australia lives, thinks, and celebrates. Food here isn't just fuel—it's a shared moment, a quiet beach picnic, a family barbecue, or a rowdy night in a city laneway. With an open mind and a curious palate, you'll find yourself tasting more than dishes—you'll be tasting the spirit of the place.

## 6.2 Australia's Coffee Culture and Local Favorites

Coffee in Australia isn't just a beverage—it's a ritual. From the moment you land in cities like Sydney or Melbourne, you'll notice it's everywhere. Not just the smell, but the devotion. Café windows proudly announce their beans and baristas by name. Locals wait in long queues without complaint for their favorite spot. And unlike many other countries, big international chains don't dominate here. Instead, independent cafés run the show, often roasting their own beans and crafting each cup with precision and pride.

If you're used to filter coffee or giant takeaway cups of sugary brew, be prepared for something very different. Australian coffee culture revolves around espresso-based drinks, crafted individually. The cornerstone of this scene is the *flat white*—a local invention that has quietly taken over the world. Picture a strong shot of espresso topped with velvety steamed milk and just a touch of foam. It's smoother than a cappuccino and bolder than a latte. You'll find it on every menu, and once you try one made right, it's hard to go back.

Most café menus stick to a familiar set of choices: espresso, long black (similar to an Americano but with a richer crema), cappuccino, latte, piccolo (a mini latte), and the beloved flat white. Many spots will also serve pour-over, Aeropress, or batch brew, especially in cities where specialty coffee is thriving. Melbourne, in particular, is famous for cafés that take their beans as seriously , offering single-origin roasts with tasting notes like "stone fruit, cocoa, and hazelnut."

Ordering coffee is easy once you get used to the rhythm. Most Australians drink their coffee in 8oz (small) or 12oz (regular) sizes. Don't expect a 20oz cup or free refills. Ask for your coffee "takeaway" instead of "to-go," and if you bring your own reusable cup, many places offer a discount of about 50 cents. Expect to pay anywhere between AUD 4.50 and 6 for a standard coffee, with specialty brews (like cold drip or single-origin espresso) priced a bit higher.

Beyond the drinks themselves, the café scene is deeply tied to lifestyle. You're not just getting coffee—you're stepping into a neighborhood's heartbeat. Tables are often full of people reading, chatting, working on laptops, or just people-watching. The vibe tends to be relaxed, design-conscious, and subtly stylish. Don't be surprised to find houseplants, exposed brick, natural light, and a laid-back playlist humming in the background. In bigger cities, dog-friendly courtyards and milk alternatives are the norm, not the exception.

One of the most distinct aspects of café life in Australia is how local everything feels. Roasters are often independent and proudly Australian—names like Five Senses, Mecca, Proud Mary, and Single O come up often in conversations among coffee lovers. Some cafés even roast their own beans in-house, filling the air with that rich, toasted scent that practically pulls you through the door.

Melbourne is often considered the capital of Australian coffee, and with good reason. Suburbs like Fitzroy, Carlton, and Brunswick are home to cafés that blend exceptional brewing with laid-back hospitality. Try Industry Beans, Patricia Coffee Brewers, or Seven Seeds for a cup that feels like an education in itself. In Sydney, Surry Hills, Newtown, and the Inner West are packed with excellent spots—places like Reuben Hills, Artificer, and Single O stand out for both their espresso and ambience.

Even outside the big cities, you'll be surprised by how high the standard is. In small towns across Tasmania, coastal Queensland, and regional South Australia, it's not unusual to find a surf shack or a converted bakery serving lattes that rival anything in the city. Australians are loyal to good coffee, and many regional cafés rise to the occasion. Look out for local favorites and don't be afraid to ask the barista for recommendations.

If you're traveling with dietary restrictions or preferences, you'll be pleased to know that almost every café offers alternatives like oat, almond, soy, and lactose-free milk. Oat milk has become particularly popular in recent years, appreciated for its creamy texture and environmental friendliness. You'll also find vegan-friendly pastries, gluten-free banana bread, and dairy-free treats widely available.

The café menus themselves often extend beyond coffee. In fact, breakfast and brunch are deeply tied to café culture. Think house-made granola with poached pears, corn fritters with avocado salsa, or miso mushrooms on sourdough toast. This is where the fusion of cultures really shines—you might see kimchi scrambled eggs or Persian feta smashed on rye with pomegranate seeds. Prices vary, but a brunch for one typically costs between AUD 18 and 25, and it's usually worth every bite.

Another beloved coffee tradition is the *drive-through café van*—especially in more rural or beachside areas. These are mobile setups, often parked beside highways or beaches, serving espresso to locals and road-trippers alike. It's a testament to how seriously Australians take their daily cup, even when far from the city grid.

For those who want to dive deeper into the scene, coffee tours and tastings are available in major cities. Some roasters offer cupping sessions (a coffee tasting method used by professionals), where you can compare different beans and learn about sourcing, roasting, and brewing. These experiences typically run between AUD 30 and 60 and give you a whole new appreciation for what's in your cup.

Even as a visitor, you'll quickly notice how much pride Australians take in their coffee scene. Conversations around coffee aren't just about flavor—they're about ethics, sustainability, and community. Many cafés source fair-trade or direct-trade beans, support local dairy suppliers, and compost their coffee grounds. There's a strong movement toward reducing waste, and you'll see reusable cups (KeepCups, especially) everywhere. If you forget yours, some cafés offer "cup swaps" or mug libraries where you borrow and return.

In cities like Canberra and Hobart, emerging coffee scenes are gaining traction too, with innovative cafés opening up in converted shipping containers, old train stations, or tucked inside bookstores. This sense of reinvention, paired with quality, is what makes Australian coffee culture so compelling—it's always evolving but never losing sight of the basics: a well-pulled shot, good milk, and a human connection over something simple and satisfying.

So whether you're sipping your morning flat white on a breezy balcony in Byron Bay, grabbing a double shot in a bustling Adelaide laneway, or enjoying a quiet afternoon cappuccino in a Tasmanian mountain town, there's a sense of ritual and community to every cup. It's not just about caffeine. It's about rhythm, quality, and the Australian way of slowing down to enjoy something done right.

## 6.3 Dietary Tips and Budgeting for Meals

Australia's food scene is as diverse as its landscapes, which makes it a pretty friendly place if you're traveling with dietary needs—or a tight budget. Whether you're vegan, gluten-free, halal, vegetarian, or just trying to keep your spending in check, you'll find plenty of ways to eat well across the country without too much stress. It all comes down to knowing where to look, how to order, and what the locals do to eat smart.

Start with the good news: Australia is generally very accommodating when it comes to dietary requirements. Most restaurants, cafés, and even takeout spots label allergens and dietary info clearly on menus. You'll often see symbols like "GF" for gluten-free or "V" for vegetarian, and staff are usually knowledgeable and happy to help. Especially in urban areas like Melbourne, Sydney, and Brisbane, it's common to find full vegan menus, organic produce, and specialty items like dairy-free cheeses or gluten-free breads.

If you're plant-based, you're in luck. The vegan movement has taken off across Australia, with dedicated vegan cafés, bakeries, and burger joints popping up in most major cities. Look for names like Lord of the Fries (a plant-based fast food chain), Green Mushroom in Sydney, or Smith & Daughters in Melbourne. Even standard cafes often have solid vegan options like avocado toast, tofu scrambles, or smoothie bowls. Expect to pay around AUD 15–25 for a hearty vegan meal in a sit-down spot, and a bit less at takeaway joints.

For gluten-free eaters, the options are wide and getting wider. Many bakeries now carry gluten-free muffins or slices, and you'll see GF pizza bases or pasta options on most Italian menus. Thai and Vietnamese cuisines, which are popular and widely available across Australia, also offer plenty of naturally gluten-free choices like rice paper rolls, noodle salads, and curries. Just double-check with staff about sauces, as soy sauce and marinades sometimes contain hidden gluten.

Halal options are also easy to find, especially in multicultural neighborhoods in cities like Sydney (Lakemba, Auburn) or Melbourne (Broadmeadows, Dandenong). You'll find Middle Eastern, Turkish, Indian, and Indonesian eateries offering halal meat, as well as halal-certified butcher shops and grocery stores. Halal Snack Packs (HSPs)—a combination of fries, doner meat, cheese, and sauce—are a popular late-night meal in urban areas and are often halal by default.

If you keep kosher, your best bet is to stick to major cities. Melbourne and Sydney both have kosher bakeries, delis, and grocery shops, mostly clustered around Jewish communities in suburbs like Caulfield or Bondi. Online directories can help you locate certified eateries, though kosher options are less common than halal.

Now, if you're watching your budget—and let's face it, eating out three times a day in Australia can add up fast—there are several tricks to keep things under control.

First, get familiar with local supermarkets. Chains like Woolworths, Coles, and Aldi are your go-tos for snacks, basic meals, and fresh produce. You'll find pre-packed sandwiches for around AUD 5–7, fruit cups, instant noodles, and microwaveable meals that are easy to prepare if your accommodation has a kitchenette or shared kitchen.

Speaking of kitchens, staying somewhere with access to one (like a hostel, serviced apartment, or Airbnb) can make a huge difference. Even making breakfast yourself—think toast, cereal, and coffee—can save you AUD 15 a day. Pick up ingredients from a local market and cook a simple pasta or stir-fry for dinner, and suddenly you're spending AUD 5–8 on a meal instead of AUD 20–30.

Another local tip: keep an eye out for lunch specials. Many restaurants, particularly Asian, Italian, or pub-style venues, offer a discounted set menu between 12 pm and 3 pm. You might score a curry and rice for AUD 10 or a sushi roll combo for AUD 12. It's a great way to enjoy a sit-down meal without breaking your budget.

RSL clubs and pubs (especially in smaller towns) also tend to offer great value meals. For around AUD 15–20, you can usually get a solid plate of chicken parmigiana, steak and chips, or fish and salad. Many also have meal deals on certain nights—like "$12 schnitzel Mondays" or "$10 burger Tuesdays"—and some even include a drink.

Don't overlook bakeries, either. Aussie bakeries are institutions, and they often serve hot savory items like meat pies, pasties, sausage rolls, and quiches at low prices (AUD 4–7). Vegetarian options are common, and vegan pastries are starting to pop up in city bakeries. Pair one with a takeaway coffee and you've got a meal under AUD 10 that'll keep you full.

For dessert or snacks, hit up supermarket chains or convenience stores like 7-Eleven. You'll find Aussie staples like Tim Tams (chocolate biscuits), Shapes (savoury crackers), and Paddle Pops (ice cream). 7-Eleven also offers coffee, hot food, and "$1 Wednesday" deals on things like pies or donuts.

Want to eat local without splurging? Farmers' markets are a good compromise. You can grab fresh fruit, pastries, and ready-to-eat meals from food trucks or stallholders. Markets in places like Byron Bay, Fremantle, or Hobart are famous for their food stalls and are perfect for an affordable, local lunch with a view.

Tap water in Australia is safe to drink everywhere, so bring a reusable bottle and refill it as you go. It'll save money and reduce waste. Many parks and public areas have refill stations.

In terms of budgeting your food overall, here's a rough idea for daily costs:

- **Budget traveler (self-catering + occasional takeout):** AUD 20–30/day
- **Mid-range traveler (1 café meal + 2 simple meals):** AUD 35–50/day
- **Dining-focused traveler (3 meals out + snacks):** AUD 70–100+/day

Of course, this varies depending on where you are. Sydney and Melbourne tend to be more expensive than smaller cities or rural areas. Tourist hotspots like Byron Bay, Broome, or Hamilton Island also come with inflated prices, especially during peak seasons.

If you're using food delivery apps like Uber Eats or Menulog, keep in mind there are delivery and service fees that can add AUD 5–10 per order. While they're convenient, it's often cheaper to walk to a takeaway shop or restaurant.

For vegetarians or vegans, apps like HappyCow can help you locate the best plant-based eateries nearby. For those on strict budgets, Facebook Marketplace and local backpacker pages often have leftover grocery giveaways or bulk food swaps, especially in hostels or shared houses.

Australia's food culture is relaxed, diverse, and welcoming—and that applies to all types of eaters and spenders. Whether you're nibbling vegan street food in a Melbourne alley or sharing a beachside barbecue with friends you just met, there's always a way to enjoy good food without overcomplicating it.

# 7. Practical Tips and Local Etiquette

## 7.1 Currency, Safety, SIM Cards, and Tipping

When you're preparing for a trip to Australia, it's easy to get caught up in planning adventures and bucket-list stops. But the practical stuff matters just as much—especially when it helps your trip run smoothly and keeps you safe and informed. Here's what you'll want to know upfront: how money works, staying connected, safety on the ground, and how to show respect in a country with a unique cultural landscape.

### Currency and Everyday Costs

Australia's official currency is the **Australian Dollar (AUD)**. Notes come in $5, $10, $20, $50, and $100, and coins are in $2, $1, 50¢, 20¢, 10¢, and 5¢ denominations. Credit and debit cards are widely accepted—even for small purchases like coffee or a tram ride—so you don't need to carry too much cash. Most Australians use "tap and go" contactless payments via card or mobile phone (Apple Pay, Google Pay), so expect a fast checkout.

ATMs are easy to find in cities and towns. Just be aware that private ATMs (like those in pubs or convenience stores) often charge higher fees. Stick to machines operated by major banks like Commonwealth, NAB, Westpac, or ANZ when you can.

As for costs, Australia isn't exactly a bargain destination, but it's manageable with some planning. Expect the following as rough daily travel prices:

- **Coffee:** AUD 4.50–6
- **Fast food meal:** AUD 10–15
- **Dinner at a mid-range restaurant:** AUD 25–45
- **Budget accommodation (hostel/private room):** AUD 40–80
- **Mid-range hotel:** AUD 120–250
- **Public transport fare (city trip):** AUD 3–5
- **Domestic flight (one-way):** AUD 100–300 depending on season and route

If you're visiting during Australian summer (December–February), especially over the Christmas holidays, prices can jump due to high demand. Booking ahead helps.

## Tipping in Australia

Tipping isn't a big part of Australian culture. Workers are paid relatively well, so there's no pressure to tip. That said, tipping for exceptional service is appreciated, especially in restaurants or on tours. A general guideline:

- **Restaurants:** Round up the bill or leave 5–10% for great service
- **Cafés:** Not expected, but you can toss coins into the tip jar
- **Taxis/Uber:** Round up to the nearest dollar
- **Tours/Guides:** AUD 5–10 per person for a half-day or AUD 10–20 for a full day

No one will glare at you if you don't tip, but a small thank-you can go a long way.

## SIM Cards and Staying Connected

Australia's mobile coverage is decent in cities and larger towns, but it can be limited or nonexistent in remote areas, especially the Outback. If you plan to venture far from cities, check your carrier's coverage map beforehand.

Buying a local SIM card is simple and will save you a lot compared to international roaming fees. Major providers are:

- **Telstra:** Best for wide coverage, including rural areas
- **Optus:** Solid coverage and often more affordable than Telstra
- **Vodafone:** Budget-friendly but weaker in regional zones

You can pick up a prepaid SIM at airports, supermarkets, or dedicated phone shops like JB Hi-Fi or Woolworths Mobile. Plans start at around AUD 10–15 for 7 days with calls, texts, and 5GB+ of data. For a month-long trip, expect to pay AUD 30–50 for a decent package with 20–60GB.

Most cafes, public libraries, airports, and even some buses and trains offer free Wi-Fi, though speeds can vary. Rural areas and national parks may have no reception at all, so download maps, reservations, and important info before heading off-grid.

## Emergency Services and Health Care

Dial **000** for all emergencies in Australia (police, fire, ambulance). The service is free, and operators are trained to assist calmly and quickly.

Travel insurance is highly recommended. While Australia has excellent healthcare, non-residents must pay out of pocket unless covered under a reciprocal agreement (available to residents of countries like the UK, New Zealand, and some EU countries). A simple GP visit can cost AUD 70–100, and hospital stays can cost thousands without coverage.

## Beach Safety and Local Warnings

Australian beaches are beautiful—but they're not always gentle. Riptides (known as "rips") are common and can be dangerous. Always swim between the red and yellow flags, which mark the patrolled area. Lifesavers are trained to help if needed, and beach signs often list hazard ratings, jellyfish warnings, or surf conditions.

In northern Australia (Queensland, Northern Territory, parts of WA), **marine stingers** like box jellyfish are a threat from October to May. During this season, wear a stinger suit when swimming or snorkelling in open water, or stick to designated enclosures.

Also, **don't touch wildlife.** Kangaroos, cassowaries, and dingoes may look cute or calm but can become aggressive if provoked. Keep a respectful distance and never feed wild animals—it's both unsafe and illegal in many areas.

## Indigenous Respect and Regional Sensitivities

Australia is home to the world's oldest continuous cultures, and many landscapes hold deep significance for Indigenous communities. When visiting sacred sites—such as **Uluru**, **Kakadu**, or **Arnhem Land**—treat them with the same reverence you'd show at a cathedral or temple.

Some specific etiquette tips:

- **Don't climb sacred sites.** For example, climbing Uluru is now officially prohibited.
- **Ask before photographing people or cultural art.**
- **Stick to marked paths and signage in Indigenous areas.**
- **Book local-led tours.** They offer richer insight and ensure your visit supports the community.

In remote communities, alcohol may be restricted or banned, and outside visitors should behave with humility and sensitivity. Always follow posted guidelines and respect local laws.

## Everyday Aussie Etiquette

Australians are friendly, informal, and big on fairness. Expect casual greetings like "G'day" or "How's it going?" even from strangers. Most interactions are laid-back and conversational—no need for overly formal language.

That said, there are a few social cues to keep in mind:

- **Queueing:** Wait your turn in line. Aussies value fairness.
- **Punctuality:** Being on time is appreciated, especially in business or group tours.
- **Dress code:** Casual is fine most of the time, but "smart casual" is expected at nicer restaurants or events.
- **Noise and manners:** In hostels, on public transport, or in national parks, keep noise levels down. Respect shared spaces.

## Outback and Regional Travel Tips

If you're planning to drive through the Outback or rural areas:

- **Plan fuel stops.** Distances can be huge, and fuel stations may be 100km+ apart.
- **Tell someone your route.** Mobile service may drop out for long stretches.
- **Carry plenty of water and snacks.** Temperatures can soar, and car breakdowns take time to resolve.
- **Wildlife warning:** Kangaroos are most active at dawn and dusk and often leap across roads. Avoid driving at these times if possible.

## Final Thoughts

Australia is easygoing and welcoming, but being prepared with the right practical knowledge helps you feel more confident and connected. Whether it's knowing how to pay for coffee, navigating regional sensitivities, or finding cell coverage in the Outback, these tips are the kind of things you'd want a savvy traveler friend to tell you before you land.

## 7.2 Local Laws and Common Cultural Norms

Every country has its own rhythm—rules and unspoken customs that shape how people live, communicate, and share space. Australia might strike you as laid-back at first, but underneath the casual smiles and sunny beaches are laws and social norms that are taken seriously. Knowing a few of these in advance can help you avoid awkward moments, misunderstandings, or even fines.

This section gives you a practical look at everyday legal expectations and cultural etiquette. It's not about memorizing the law book—just the kind of helpful advice you'd want from someone who's lived there and understands how things work.

**Respect the Law: What Travelers Should Know**

Australia has clear and well-enforced laws. Police officers are approachable, but they don't overlook rule-breaking. Even minor offenses can carry on-the-spot fines, so here's what you need to keep in mind:

**1. Alcohol Laws and BYO**

Drinking  is usually not allowed .

On the flip side, **BYO (Bring Your Own)** is a common practice in many restaurants, especially Asian and casual places.

## 2. Drug Laws

Recreational drugs are illegal across Australia. Even small quantities of cannabis can lead to fines or arrest, depending on the state. Drug use, possession, or supply can have serious legal consequences, and travelers are not exempt from local enforcement.

## 3. Smoking and Vaping

Smoking is banned in enclosed public spaces, including restaurants, bars, offices, airports, and public transport. Many outdoor public areas like beaches, parks, and playgrounds are also smoke-free. This extends to vaping as well.

Always look for signage. Fines can range from AUD 200 to over AUD 1000 for smoking in prohibited areas.

## 4. Driving Laws

If you plan to drive in Australia, know this:

- **Drive on the left-hand side.**
- Seatbelts are mandatory for all passengers.
- Speed limits are strictly enforced, with hidden cameras and radar used regularly.
- Using a mobile phone while driving (unless hands-free) is illegal.

Foreign licenses are accepted, but some states require an **International Driving Permit (IDP)** if your license isn't in English. Double-check with the rental agency and your state of arrival.

## 5. Littering and Waste

Australia is clean for a reason. Littering, including cigarette butts or gum, can result in heavy fines. Cities like Sydney and Melbourne are equipped with CCTV that monitors public behavior. If you're camping or road-tripping, take all waste with you and follow Leave No Trace principles.

## Cultural Norms: What's Considered Rude, Casual, or Kind

Australia's social culture might feel familiar, especially if you come from an English-speaking country. But a few unwritten rules can catch visitors off guard.

## 1. Casual Doesn't Mean Careless

Yes, Australians are relaxed and informal. You'll hear "mate" tossed around a lot, even from strangers. First names are used quickly, and small talk is light and easy. But don't confuse casualness with a lack of boundaries—respect and fairness are highly valued.

Interrupting others, bragging, or acting entitled will quickly rub people the wrong way. It's better to be friendly, humble, and open to conversation.

## 2. Punctuality Still Matters

Being "fashionably late" isn't really a thing in Australia. Whether it's a dinner reservation, guided tour, or meetup with a local friend, being on time shows respect. If you're running late, even for informal plans, a quick message or call is appreciated.

## 3. Tipping is Modest

As mentioned earlier, tipping is not obligatory but appreciated in certain situations. Australians don't tip to impress—they do it as a small thank-you when service goes above and beyond.

## 4. Personal Space and Queueing

Standing too close to strangers or cutting in line is frowned upon. Australians take queuing seriously—whether it's for a coffee, bus, or ATM. Be aware of your space, especially in smaller towns where things move at a slower pace.

## 5. Conversation Topics

Australians are open-minded, but politics, religion, and personal finances aren't usually brought up in casual conversation. It's fine to ask questions, but do so with respect and curiosity—not judgment or assumption.

Also, **don't joke about stereotypes**. Joking about kangaroos in the streets or making fun of accents may not be received well, especially if you're new to the country.

## 6. Indigenous Culture and Awareness

Respect for Aboriginal and Torres Strait Islander peoples is growing, but there's still a long way to go in national healing. Many Australians are aware of this history, and visitors are encouraged to be thoughtful and informed.

Avoid calling sacred sites "empty" or describing cultural art as "primitive." If you're not sure what's respectful, join a local-led Indigenous tour, read signage carefully, and listen before asking questions.

## Other Local Rules and Regional Quirks

## 1. Beach Culture Comes with Rules

Australia's beach life is iconic, but it runs on unwritten codes:

- Always swim between the red and yellow flags.
- Don't bring glass containers to the sand.

- Cover up when leaving the beach—it's fine to walk barefoot, but walking into shops in a swimsuit isn't considered polite.
- Sunscreen is essential. Locals reapply constantly, and you should too.

## 2. Clothing and Dress

Most Australians dress casually. Flip-flops (thongs), shorts, and T-shirts are everyday wear, even in cities. However, in restaurants or theater venues, "smart casual" means closed-toe shoes, neat pants, or a sundress. A good rule of thumb: if you're not sure, dress one notch neater than the locals.

## 3. Respect the Rules of the Road

Jaywalking is technically illegal in Australia. If you cross a road outside the marked crosswalk or during a red pedestrian signal, you could be fined (especially in major cities like Sydney). Police occasionally enforce this, especially near transport hubs.

## 4. Noise and Late Nights

Australians value peace, especially in residential areas. If you're staying in an Airbnb or hotel, keep talking after 10pm. Many places have noise curfews, and neighbors won't hesitate to make a complaint.

## Final Thought: It's Not About Being Perfect—Just Being Aware

Australia is easy to love—and easy to enjoy when you respect the local rhythm. It's not about rules for the sake of rules. Most of these laws and norms exist to keep life fair, respectful, and safe for everyone—locals and visitors alike.

When in doubt, watch what locals do, stay humble, and ask questions kindly. Australians are happy to help, especially when they see that you're trying to do the right thing.

# 7.3 Health and Emergency Services

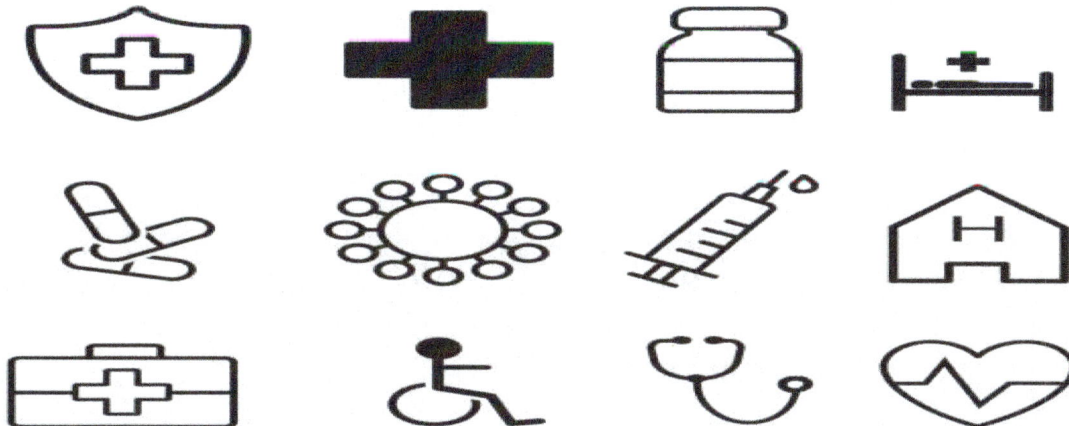

Traveling across Australia is generally low-risk when it comes to health and safety, but like anywhere in the world, it pays to be prepared. Whether you're planning a short city stay or a month-long outback adventure, knowing how to access medical care, understanding the public and private healthcare systems, and being ready for emergencies gives you peace of mind.

This guide walks you through everything you need to know about staying healthy on the road, accessing emergency help, and what to expect if something goes wrong.

## 1. Australia's Healthcare System: What Travelers Should Know

Australia has a world-class healthcare system, and its public facilities are high-quality, clean, and efficient. The public system, known as **Medicare**, is mostly for Australian citizens and residents, but visitors from certain countries with **Reciprocal Health Care Agreements (RHCA)**—like the UK, New Zealand, Ireland, and a few European nations—may be eligible for limited care under this program. Everyone else should have travel insurance to cover both emergency and routine medical care.

Even if you're young, healthy, or just passing through, **travel health insurance is non-negotiable**. A simple hospital visit can cost hundreds, while an emergency evacuation from a remote area can reach thousands of dollars.

**Key takeaway:** Don't count on "figuring it out later." Health care is accessible, but costs without coverage can add up quickly.

### 2. Accessing Medical Help: Who to Call, Where to Go

Australia has a straightforward emergency response system and easy access to general healthcare services. Here's what you need to know:

**In an Emergency:**
Dial **000** (triple zero) for **ambulance, police, or fire** services. This is a free call from any phone.

**If You're Sick, But It's Not an Emergency:**
You can go to a **General Practitioner (GP)**—a local doctor who handles non-emergency health concerns. GP clinics are found in every city, suburb, and town. Some accept walk-ins, others require appointments.

**Out-of-Hours Clinics:**
Many cities have after-hours medical centers open late or on weekends. If you're not near one, you can call a **national health advice line** at **1800 022 222**, which connects you to registered nurses who can advise you on next steps.

**Pharmacies (Chemists):**
Pharmacists in Australia are highly trained and often your first stop for minor issues—think colds, bites, allergies, or traveler's tummy. Many pharmacies are open late, especially in metro areas.

**Hospitals and Emergency Departments:**
All major cities have excellent public hospitals with 24/7 emergency departments. If you're in a rural area, you'll find smaller regional hospitals and clinics. Some remote zones are supported by **Royal Flying Doctor Service (RFDS)**, which provides emergency air evacuation if needed.

### 3. Common Travel Health Concerns

Australia doesn't pose major health risks to travelers, but here are a few issues that commonly pop up:

**Sun Exposure:**
The sun here is intense—some of the highest UV levels in the world. Sunburn happens fast, even on cloudy days.

- Always wear sunscreen (SPF 30+ minimum)
- Reapply every 2 hours, especially if swimming or sweating

- Wear a hat, sunglasses, and light long-sleeved clothing

## Dehydration:

If you're hiking, exploring national parks, or road-tripping in hot areas, dehydration creeps in quicker than you'd think.

- Carry water—at least 2–3 liters per person per day
- Add electrolyte tablets if sweating heavily
- Don't wait to feel thirsty to drink

## Mosquito-Borne Illnesses:

Diseases like **Ross River virus** and **Dengue** can appear in northern Queensland, especially during the wet season (November–April). Use insect repellent with DEET, wear long clothing at dusk, and sleep with nets or screens in tropical areas.

## Food and Water Safety:

Australia has excellent food safety standards. Tap water is safe to drink everywhere unless a sign says otherwise (which can happen in remote or desert areas).

## Allergies & Special Diets:

Restaurants are generally good at accommodating food allergies. If you have a serious allergy (e.g., nuts, shellfish), consider carrying a medical alert card or bracelet, and always let staff know clearly. For anaphylaxis, bring **epinephrine (EpiPen)** and a backup.

## 4. Mental Health and Emotional Wellbeing

Travel can be emotionally overwhelming, especially during long solo trips or after facing culture shock or minor mishaps. Australians take mental health seriously, and help is available if you need it.

## Free helplines for travelers and visitors:

- **Lifeline Australia:** 13 11 14 (available 24/7)
- **Beyond Blue:** 1300 224 636
- **Mental Health Access Line:** Available in each state, offering crisis support and advice

You can also speak to a GP for referrals to counseling or therapy.

## 5. Medications: Bringing and Buying

If you're traveling with **prescription medication**, bring enough for your full stay, along with a **doctor's letter** explaining your medical condition and the medication's purpose. Medicines must be in original packaging.

Australia has **strict import rules on medications**. Some drugs commonly used overseas (like codeine-based painkillers) are restricted or controlled here.

If you need a refill while in the country, you'll need to visit a GP first. Not all foreign prescriptions can be filled directly.

**Tip:** Check your medication status on the Australian Government's [Therapeutic Goods Administration (TGA)](#) website before travel.

### 6. Insurance Tips: What to Look For

When buying travel insurance, make sure it includes:

- Hospital care and doctor visits
- Emergency evacuation (especially for remote travel)
- Pre-existing conditions (if needed)
- Coverage for adventure activities like diving, hiking, or surfing
- Trip interruption or delays (in case of medical emergencies)

Compare providers carefully. Many Australian insurers like **Cover-More**, **NIB**, or **Southern Cross** also cater to international travelers.

### 7. Health Tips by Region

**Tropical North Queensland (Cairns, Daintree, Cape Tribulation):**
High humidity, mosquito risk, and jellyfish stingers in the ocean from November to May. Wear a stinger suit when swimming and use insect repellent.

**Outback and Red Centre (Uluru, Alice Springs):**
Extremely dry and hot in summer, with long distances between help. Carry first-aid supplies, water, and satellite phones if venturing far off-track.

**Major Cities (Sydney, Melbourne, Brisbane):**
Easy access to care, 24/7 pharmacies, and high-standard hospitals. Some public holidays may reduce clinic hours.

**Tasmania and Southern Australia:**
Cooler, with fewer heat-related risks, but sudden weather changes can bring hypothermia risk in remote hikes—always check weather forecasts.

### 8. Emergency Essentials to Pack

- First-aid kit (band-aids, antiseptic, painkillers, antihistamines)
- Any prescription medication with doctor's note
- Sunscreen and lip balm with SPF
- Rehydration salts or tablets
- Insect repellent
- Copies of your travel insurance and emergency contacts

### Final Word: Don't Panic—Just Be Prepared

Australia is one of the safest and most medically accessible countries in the world. With some basic preparation and awareness, you'll be well equipped to handle everything from minor colds to more serious emergencies.

Use common sense, stay hydrated, wear sunscreen, and know where the closest help is—whether it's a pharmacy on a city corner or a clinic hours away in the Outback.

If something does go wrong, don't hesitate to ask for help. Australians are known for their friendliness, and support systems are in place to make sure travelers are looked after, wherever they are.

## 7.4 Indigenous Culture: Respect and Learning

Australia is home to one of the oldest living cultures in the world, with over 65,000 years of continuous connection to land, language, story, and tradition. The Aboriginal and Torres Strait Islander peoples—across hundreds of distinct nations and language groups—offer not only historical depth but ongoing cultural richness that shapes modern Australia in subtle and powerful ways. As a traveler, approaching this culture with curiosity, humility, and respect opens the door to some of the most meaningful experiences the country has to offer.

This section is your guide to engaging thoughtfully with Indigenous culture, understanding key protocols, and recognizing how to be a respectful visitor.

### Start with Respect: You Are on Country

Everywhere you step in Australia is Indigenous land. Whether you're walking along the cliffs of the Sydney coast, hiking through Uluru's red heart, or driving through eucalyptus forest in Victoria, you are on Country—an idea that means more than just land. In Aboriginal worldview, "Country" is alive. It holds ancestral knowledge, spirits, stories, and responsibilities. It's not something people own, but something people belong to.

Wherever you go, learn which Traditional Owners care for that place. Many tour guides, plaques, and visitor centers now acknowledge the local custodians at the beginning of a talk or trail, such as "the Gadigal people of the Eora Nation" in Sydney or "the Anangu people" in Uluru-Kata Tjuta. Listening to these names isn't just a formality—it's a reminder that the land has history far deeper than colonial timelines.

## What you can do:

- Acknowledge Traditional Owners when you enter a new place
- Learn the local Indigenous name for landmarks (e.g., Uluru instead of Ayers Rock)
- Avoid using past tense—these cultures are living, not relics

## Cultural Protocols: What to Know Before You Go

Some Indigenous areas—particularly sacred sites—come with specific protocols, and it's essential to follow them. This isn't about tourism rules; it's about cultural respect.

## Examples of common protocols:

- **Photography Restrictions:** Some places request that no photos be taken out of respect for sacred stories or cultural privacy. Always read signage or ask.
- **Don't Climb Sacred Sites:** Uluru, for instance, is not to be climbed. While it was once permitted, traditional owners ask visitors to walk around it instead. Honoring that request is a simple act of solidarity.
- **Gender-Specific Knowledge:** Some stories or sites are meant only for men or women within the culture. If this is mentioned during a tour, respect it and don't press for details.
- **No Trespassing on Closed Land:** Certain lands are privately owned or closed off during ceremonies. Respect no-entry signs, even in remote areas.

**Tip:** When in doubt, ask. Most Indigenous hosts are happy to explain what's appropriate and why.

## Cultural Experiences Led by First Nations Guides

One of the best ways to learn is through direct experience. Across Australia, you'll find tours, workshops, and performances led by Indigenous people eager to share their knowledge and connection to the country.

**Popular experiences include:**

- **Dot painting workshops** in the Red Centre
- **Bush tucker walks** in the Daintree Rainforest, where guides point out edible plants, medicinal uses, and traditional gathering techniques
- **Dreamtime storytelling** sessions near sacred sites
- **Cultural performances** at places like Tjapukai Aboriginal Cultural Park (Cairns) or the Aboriginal Centre for the Performing Arts (Brisbane)
- **Welcome to Country or Smoking Ceremonies** at festivals or community gatherings

**What you gain:** A new perspective on the land, deeper understanding of local history, and a more human connection to the people who have cared for these places for millennia.

**What they gain:** Support for community-run businesses, economic empowerment, and cultural preservation.

### Language and Identity: Be Aware of Terminology

Language matters. Here are a few respectful guidelines when referring to Indigenous Australians:

- Say **Aboriginal and Torres Strait Islander peoples** when referring to both major groups. Use **First Nations peoples** as a respectful alternative.
- Avoid "Aborigines" or "the Aboriginals"—these terms are outdated and can be offensive.
- Use **people**, not tribes.
- Refer to a person's **language group or nation** if known (e.g., Wiradjuri, Yolŋu, Noongar).
- Understand that **Torres Strait Islanders** are distinct from mainland Aboriginal peoples and have their own cultures, languages, and history.

**Tip:** If someone shares their background or identity with you, listen carefully and reflect it back respectfully.

### Indigenous Art: From Gallery Walls to Red Earth

Australia's Indigenous art scene is world-renowned, and not just because of its visual beauty. Each dot, line, and color often tells stories—of ancestors, seasons, journeys, and law. It's deeply symbolic, passed through generations, and tied to specific knowledge.

You'll see art in many forms:

- Dot paintings from Central Desert artists
- Bark paintings in Arnhem Land
- Carvings and woven baskets in the Top End
- Contemporary murals on city walls
- Massive collaborative works in galleries like the **National Gallery of Australia** or **Art Gallery of NSW**

**Buying art:** Choose ethically. Buy from Aboriginal-owned art centers or galleries that support fair pay and cultural integrity. Labels like **Indigenous Art Code** help identify responsible sellers.

**Never reproduce or copy sacred designs**, even if you're just doodling in a notebook. These motifs carry deep cultural meaning.

### Indigenous-Led Conservation and Eco-Tourism

Across Australia, Indigenous rangers play a key role in protecting land, fire management, wildlife conservation, and sustainable tourism. Parks like **Kakadu**, **Nitmiluk**, **Purnululu**, and **Daintree** are co-managed by Indigenous owners and national agencies.

By visiting these parks, attending ranger talks, or joining cultural walks, you support efforts to keep both ecosystems and culture thriving.

### What you can do:

- Attend **free ranger-led activities** in national parks
- Respect fire bans and local environmental guidance
- Donate or volunteer with Indigenous-led land conservation projects

### Being a Thoughtful Guest: Everyday Actions That Matter

You don't need a tour or museum ticket to practice respect. Some of the most important moments come in small choices:

- **Pause at an Acknowledgment of Country** rather than brushing it off
- **Buy directly from Indigenous makers** at local markets
- **Listen without interrupting** when someone shares cultural knowledge
- **Learn a few local words**, even if it's just "hello" or "thank you"
- **Question stereotypes** you may have seen in the media
- **Teach others** what you've learned when you return home

### Final Thought: Culture Is Ongoing, Not Frozen in Time

Indigenous culture in Australia is not stuck in the past. It's living, adapting, and vibrant. Today's First Nations communities include artists, politicians, scientists, surfers, farmers, and elders. Engaging with this culture means acknowledging its history—yes—but also recognizing its modern voice and future.

If you approach each encounter with a sense of learning, openness, and gratitude, your journey through Australia won't just be about landscapes. It will be about people. And that's where the real heart of travel lives.

# 8. Sample Itineraries and Planning Tools

## 8.1 Classic 7-Day East Coast Highlights

There's something unforgettable about moving down Australia's East Coast—from the urban sparkle of Sydney to the tropical warmth of Cairns. This 7-day itinerary blends city charm, coastal beauty, and natural wonder. Whether you're traveling in summer or winter, this plan gives you the best of beaches, wildlife, reef, and rainforest, while keeping your days manageable and full of memorable moments.

**Day 1: Arrive in Sydney – Harborside Welcome**

Touch down in Sydney and head straight for the city's heart—Circular Quay. You'll be welcomed by the Opera House and Harbour Bridge, two icons that instantly anchor you in Australia. If arriving early, take the coastal ferry to Manly for a scenic introduction or stroll through The Rocks for history and hidden pubs.

- **Travel Tip:** A taxi from the airport to central Sydney costs about AUD $50. The Airport Link train is faster and cheaper, around AUD $20.
- **Evening:** Grab a bite in Darling Harbour or Barangaroo. Expect mains around AUD $25–$35.

**Day 2: Bondi to Coogee Coastal Walk and City Views**

Begin the day with a sunrise walk along the Bondi to Coogee trail. It's about 6 kilometers of coastal cliffs, ocean pools, and beach life—great year-round but especially refreshing from September to April. In the afternoon, head to the Sydney Tower Eye for sweeping views or join a guided tour of the Opera House.

- **Activity Ideas:**
  - Bondi Icebergs Pool (AUD $10 entry)
  - Opera House Tour (AUD $43 per adult)
- **Evening Suggestion:** Dine in Surry Hills or Newtown for trendy eats and people-watching.

## Day 3: Fly to Brisbane – Explore the River City

Book a morning flight to Brisbane (1.5 hours) and settle into the relaxed pace of Queensland's capital. Walk along South Bank, take a dip at the man-made Streets Beach, or catch river views from the CityCat ferry.

- **Transport Tip:** Budget airlines like Jetstar or Virgin often have Sydney–Brisbane flights for under AUD $120.
- **Local Gem:** Visit the Queensland Art Gallery and Gallery of Modern Art (GOMA)—both free.

## Day 4: Day Trip to the Gold Coast or Moreton Island

Choose your adventure. You can train down to the Gold Coast for a beach day in Surfers Paradise or take a ferry to Moreton Island for snorkeling and dolphin watching.

- **Costs:**
  - Return train to Gold Coast: AUD $12–$15
  - Moreton Island day trip tours: Around AUD $150–$200 including ferry, lunch, and activities.
- **Tip:** Summer is ideal for island trips, while winter offers mild, sunny days on the coast.

## Day 5: Fly to Cairns – Gateway to the Reef

Head north with a morning flight to Cairns (about 2.5 hours). The city feels like a tropical gateway, with palm-lined streets and reef boats lining the marina. Take the rest of the day to unwind, walk the Esplanade, and swim in the public lagoon.

- **Flight Range:** AUD $130–$200 depending on the season.
- **Evening:** Try fresh seafood or a local favorite like kangaroo steak. Mains range from AUD $20–$40.

### Day 6: Great Barrier Reef Adventure

Spend the day on or under the water. Book a full-day snorkeling or diving tour out to the outer reef. Most tours leave around 8 AM and return by 4 PM, offering stops at multiple reefs, lunch onboard, and guided experiences.

- **Tour Price:** Expect to pay AUD $220–$280 for a quality reef tour.
- **What to Bring:** Reef-safe sunscreen, towel, and underwater camera (some boats rent them out).

### Day 7: Rainforest or Return

Your final day can go two ways: adventure or reflection. If flying out late or staying longer, consider a half-day trip to the Daintree Rainforest or the Skyrail Rainforest Cableway to Kuranda. If heading home, take it easy with one last walk along the water and grab a coffee from a Cairns café before your flight.

- **Kuranda Skyrail Return:** Around AUD $88 per adult.
- **Daintree Tour:** From AUD $170, usually includes pickup, lunch, and a guide.

### Optional Notes:

- **Summer (Dec–Feb):** Great for beach and reef adventures, but humid in Queensland. Be ready for afternoon storms.
- **Winter (June–Aug):** Ideal for dry, sunny days in the tropics and pleasant sightseeing in the cities.

### Estimated Trip Budget (Mid-range):

- **Flights (3 domestic):** AUD $350–$500
- **Accommodation (3-star hotels or private rooms):** AUD $120–$200 per night
- **Meals and Snacks:** AUD $50–$80 per day
- **Tours and Entry Fees:** AUD $400–$600 total
- **Transport and Extras:** AUD $150–$200

## 8.2 10-Day Road Trip: From Sydney to Melbourne

A Sydney-to-Melbourne road trip is one of Australia's most rewarding drives, offering a mix of buzzing coastal towns, national parks, surf beaches, wildlife encounters, and scenic hinterlands. With ten days, you'll have enough time to take the coastal route and really soak in the diversity along the way.

### Day 1: Start in Sydney – City Sights and Last-Minute Prep

Before hitting the road, spend one last day in Sydney gathering supplies and enjoying final highlights. Walk through The Rocks, have brunch in Paddington, or stretch your legs along the Bondi to Bronte walk.

- **Tip:** Stock up on snacks, refill your water bottles, and check your car's fuel and tire pressure.
- **Rental Reminder:** Car or campervan rentals start at around AUD $60–$100 per day for economy models. Pick up from Sydney Airport or downtown.

### Day 2: Sydney to Jervis Bay (3 hours)

Leave the city via the scenic Grand Pacific Drive. Stop at the Sea Cliff Bridge near Stanwell Park, then pass through Kiama to see the blowhole before arriving in Jervis Bay. Spend the afternoon exploring Hyams Beach—famous for its powder-white sand—or paddleboarding in Booderee National Park.

- **Accommodation:** Beachfront cottages or motels (AUD $130–$200/night).
- **Food Tip:** Huskisson has some great seafood spots.

### Day 3: Jervis Bay to Batemans Bay (2.5 hours)

Cruise farther south to Batemans Bay, making stops at Murramarang National Park to spot kangaroos on the beach or enjoy a short coastal walk. If you're into oysters, Clyde River offers some of the freshest around.

- **Budget Tip:** Consider camping at one of the holiday parks for AUD $30–$50 per site.
- **Optional Activity:** Kayaking or dolphin cruises (AUD $60–$90).

### Day 4: Batemans Bay to Narooma (2.5 hours)

Continue the relaxed pace down to Narooma, a quiet gem known for turquoise waters and the chance to snorkel with seals at Montague Island. Rent snorkel gear or book a boat trip from the marina.

- **Activity Cost:** Snorkeling tours average AUD $120–$140.
- **Evening:** Dine by the water. Local pubs often have fresh catch specials.

### Day 5: Narooma to Merimbula (2.5 hours)

Wind along the Sapphire Coast and land in Merimbula—a town that feels both peaceful and playful. Go for a dip at Bar Beach or take the Merimbula Boardwalk around the lake. The oysters here are also legendary.

- **Stay:** Boutique B&Bs or caravan parks with cabins.
- **Note:** This is a great place to relax at the halfway mark.

## Day 6: Merimbula to Lakes Entrance (4 hours)

Cross into Victoria today. The drive to Lakes Entrance takes you into the heart of Gippsland, a region dotted with rivers, forests, and hidden lakes. Once there, walk the Ninety Mile Beach or book a boat cruise through the lakes system.

- **Fuel Tip:** Some stretches between towns are long—top up at Orbost.
- **Dinner:** Grab fish and chips and eat by the waterfront.

## Day 7: Lakes Entrance to Wilsons Promontory (3.5 hours)

This stretch takes you inland through rolling countryside before arriving at Wilsons Promontory National Park, known locally as "The Prom." It's one of Victoria's best-kept secrets, filled with rugged peaks, wildlife, and beaches.

- **Must-do:** Hike to Squeaky Beach or Mount Oberon for panoramic views.
- **Campgrounds:** Book well ahead, especially in summer (AUD $30–$50/night).

## Day 8: Wilsons Promontory to Phillip Island (3 hours)

Leave early and arrive at Phillip Island with plenty of time to explore. Visit the Koala Conservation Reserve, take a walk on the boardwalks at The Nobbies, and don't miss the famous Penguin Parade at sunset.

- **Penguin Parade Tickets:** AUD $30–$60 depending on seating tier.
- **Accommodation Range:** AUD $120–$250, with cozy beach cabins and eco-stays available.

## Day 9: Phillip Island to Melbourne (2 hours)

Ease into city life again by driving into Melbourne. Depending on your arrival time, start with a tram ride down Swanston Street, coffee in Fitzroy, or an afternoon in the Royal Botanic Gardens.

- **Parking Note:** Try Parkopedia or apps like EasyPark to find cheap city parking.
- **Stay:** Choose from city apartments, hotels, or quirky laneway studios (AUD $150–$300/night).

## Day 10: Explore Melbourne

Spend your final day soaking in the city's rhythm. Explore street art in Hosier Lane, sip world-class espresso in a hidden café, or shop the stalls at Queen Victoria Market. If you have time, hop on a tram to St Kilda for beachside vibes and sunset on the pier.

- **Optional Add-On:** A guided street art or food tour (AUD $40–$90).

- **Transit Tip:** Get a Myki card for local trams and trains. Daily cap is around AUD $10.

**Seasonal Tips:**

- **Summer (Dec–Feb):** Great for beach stops and longer days, but book accommodations early.
- **Winter (June–Aug):** Cooler temps in the south but still pleasant, with fewer crowds.

**Approximate Trip Budget (Mid-range):**

- **Car Rental (10 days):** AUD $600–$900
- **Accommodation:** AUD $1,200–$1,800
- **Fuel & Tolls:** AUD $250–$350
- **Food & Drinks:** AUD $500–$700
- **Activities & Entry Fees:** AUD $300–$500
- **Total Estimate:** AUD $2,850–$4,250 (per couple or solo traveler)

## 8.3 14-Day Nature & Wildlife Journey

This 14-day journey is made for nature lovers. You'll move from coastal cliffs to ancient rainforests, snorkel with marine life, meet kangaroos and koalas, and walk through deserts that hum with silence. It's a slower, immersive way to connect with Australia's wild side—without rushing or overpacking your days.

### Day 1: Arrive in Cairns – Tropical Gateway

Fly into Cairns, your launch point into North Queensland. Settle into your hotel and take an evening stroll on the Esplanade Boardwalk. Watch the sky fade behind the mangroves and try fresh barramundi at a nearby seafood grill.

- **Flight cost:** From Sydney/Melbourne ~AUD $120–$250 one-way
- **Stay:** Central hotel or eco-lodge (AUD $120–$250)

### Day 2: Snorkeling the Great Barrier Reef

Join a full-day snorkeling or diving tour out to the reef. Expect coral gardens, green sea turtles, and maybe even reef sharks. Many boats leave from Cairns Marina early in the morning and include lunch.

- **Tour cost:** AUD $180–$250 (includes gear, lunch)
- **Tip:** Pack reef-safe sunscreen and bring a waterproof camera

### Day 3: Daintree Rainforest and Cape Tribulation

Drive north toward the Daintree—a 100-million-year-old rainforest where cassowaries roam and tree frogs chirp at night. Cross the Daintree River by ferry, take a guided walk, and cool off in freshwater swimming holes.

- **Daintree River ferry:** ~AUD $45 return
- **Stay:** Jungle lodge or rainforest cabin (AUD $100–$220)

### Day 4: Wildlife Cruise and Drive to Atherton Tablelands

Take a morning river cruise to spot crocs and kingfishers, then drive inland to the cooler Atherton Tablelands. Visit waterfalls, crater lakes, and stop by a local wildlife sanctuary.

- **Highlight:** Paronella Park or Millaa Millaa Falls
- **Stay:** Farmstay or eco-cabin (AUD $90–$180)

### Day 5: Fly to Darwin and Rest

Return to Cairns and catch a flight to Darwin (around 2.5 hours). Rest up for your Top End adventure. Stroll through Darwin's waterfront and enjoy the sunset from the Mindil Beach Markets if timing works out.

- **Flight:** AUD $150–$300
- **Stay:** Central hotel or tropical guesthouse (AUD $100–$200)

### Day 6: Kakadu National Park

Rent a car or join a small group tour to explore Kakadu. Stop at Ubirr or Nourlangie for Aboriginal rock art and sweeping floodplain views. Take a late-afternoon billabong cruise for crocs and birds.

- **Park pass:** AUD $25 (valid 7 days)
- **Stay:** Lodge near Jabiru or glamping (AUD $120–$280)

### Day 7: Kakadu to Katherine Gorge (Nitmiluk)

Drive south to Katherine. Hike in Nitmiluk National Park or take a boat tour through the gorge's red cliffs. Evening is a great time for wallaby sightings.

- **Activity cost:** Gorge cruise ~AUD $95
- **Stay:** Riverside campground or lodge (AUD $80–$180)

### Day 8: Edith Falls and Return to Darwin

On your way back, cool off at Edith Falls—safe for swimming in the dry season (May–Oct). Arrive in Darwin by evening and get ready for your next flight.

- **Fuel Tip:** Distances are long—fill up at Katherine or Pine Creek.

## Day 9: Fly to Alice Springs

Take a morning flight to Alice Springs. Spend the afternoon at Alice Springs Desert Park, where you can see native reptiles, birds of prey, and learn about Aboriginal culture.

- **Flight:** AUD $150–$300
- **Stay:** Outback motel or eco-lodge (AUD $100–$200)

## Day 10: Road Trip to Kings Canyon

Drive through desert landscapes to Watarrka National Park (Kings Canyon). Stop at road stations along the way for fuel and snacks. Arrive in time for a sunset canyon rim walk or relax with views.

- **Drive time:** ~5 hours
- **Stay:** Kings Canyon Resort or campground (AUD $140–$280)

## Day 11: Kings Canyon to Uluru

Hike the canyon early in the morning, then continue the drive to Uluru-Kata Tjuta National Park. Spend the evening watching the rock change color at sunset.

- **Park pass:** AUD $38 (valid 3 days)
- **Stay:** Yulara village resort, hostel, or campground

## Day 12: Uluru and Kata Tjuta

Wake up early to catch the sunrise at Uluru, then explore Kata Tjuta's Valley of the Winds. Respect local customs by not climbing Uluru. Visit the Cultural Centre for stories and art.

- **Guided walk:** Optional ranger tours are free with entry

## Day 13: Fly to Hobart, Tasmania

Return to Alice Springs and fly to Hobart (via Melbourne). Once you land, get a feel for the quiet charm of Tasmania's capital.

- **Flight (Alice–Hobart):** AUD $200–$400
- **Stay:** Waterfront inn or eco-cabin (AUD $100–$180)

## Day 14: Bonorong Wildlife Sanctuary and Mount Wellington

Visit Bonorong to hand-feed kangaroos and meet wombats, quolls, and Tasmanian devils. In the afternoon, drive up Mount Wellington for sweeping views of the city and coastline.

- **Entry to Bonorong:** AUD $36
- **Final Dinner Idea:** Try a local seafood pub or woodfired pizza in Battery Point

**Trip Summary & Costs (Mid-range per traveler):**

- **Flights:** AUD $800–$1,200
- **Accommodation (13 nights):** AUD $1,400–$2,200
- **Tours & Park Entry:** AUD $700–$1,000
- **Food & Miscellaneous:** AUD $600–$800
- **Total Estimate:** ~AUD $3,500–$5,200

## 8.4 Seasonal Trips: Summer vs Winter Experiences

Planning a trip to Australia means thinking beyond the calendar months you're used to. Because of its size and diverse climates, what counts as summer in one region might feel like spring—or even snow—in another. Australia's summer (December to February) and winter (June to August) offer entirely different travel opportunities. Here's how to plan seasonal trips that align with your interests, whether you're chasing beaches or crisp mountain air.

Option A: Summer Adventure (December–February)

Perfect for beach lovers, snorkelers, and those seeking vibrant cities in full swing.

### Day 1–3: Sydney Sizzle
Start your journey in Sydney where summer means packed beaches and outdoor energy. Bondi, Manly, and Coogee are buzzing with surfers and sunbathers. Take the coastal walk and enjoy evening cocktails with a sea breeze.

- **What to pack:** Sun protection, sandals, reusable water bottle
- **Rough costs:** Hotel from AUD $150/night, public transport ~AUD $25/day with Opal card

### Day 4–6: Byron Bay & Hinterland
Fly or road-trip north to Byron Bay. Join morning yoga on the sand, snorkel at Julian Rocks, and browse artisan markets. Hike inland through rainforest waterfalls in Nightcap National Park.

- **Flight from Sydney to Ballina:** From AUD $90
- **Accommodation:** Eco-resorts or beach cabins (~AUD $100–$200)

### Day 7–10: Great Barrier Reef & Daintree Rainforest
Continue north to Cairns. Spend a day on the reef, another in the Daintree, and a third cooling off in the Tablelands waterfalls.

- **Seasonal tip:** December–February is the "wet season" in Far North Queensland, expect humid days and tropical storms—great for lush green scenery, but bring bug spray and a rain jacket

### Day 11–14: Melbourne Summer Vibes
Fly south to Melbourne to finish. The city is buzzing with festivals like Midsumma and open-air cinemas. Spend afternoons in laneway cafés or day trips to the Mornington Peninsula for coastal views and hot springs.

- **Flight from Cairns to Melbourne:** AUD $150–$250
- **Weather:** Dry, sunny days (25–35°C)

Option B: Winter Escape (June–August)

Ideal for hikers, wildlife seekers, and those who prefer cool, crisp air with fewer crowds.

### Day 1–3: Tasmania's Wilderness
Begin in Hobart and head to Freycinet or Cradle Mountain. With snow on peaks and fog over eucalyptus groves, it's quiet, wild, and serene. Perfect for hiking and spotting wallabies or wombats.

- **Weather:** 0–12°C; pack thermals and a waterproof jacket
- **Costs:** Park pass ~AUD $40; cabins ~AUD $120/night

### Day 4–6: Red Centre – Uluru and Kings Canyon
Fly to Alice Springs. Winter is the most comfortable time to visit the desert. Hike Kings Canyon at dawn and experience Uluru at golden hour without the heat exhaustion.

- **High season:** June–August is peak for the Outback, so book early
- **Daytime temps:** 18–25°C, but nights drop below freezing

### Day 7–9: Kangaroo Island (South Australia)
Take a short flight or ferry to Kangaroo Island. Winter is the season for whale watching and wildlife spotting. Seals bask on beaches, and echidnas wander trails.

- **Costs:** Ferry ~AUD $100 return per person; car hire essential (~AUD $90/day)

### Day 10–14: Blue Mountains & Snowy Mountains
Wrap your trip with cooler alpine regions. Start near Sydney with hikes in the Blue

Mountains—misty valleys, gum trees, and waterfalls. Then head to the Snowy Mountains if you're keen on skiing or snowboarding.

- **Thredbo and Perisher (NSW) ski passes:** From AUD $140/day
- **Alternative:** Cozy mountain lodges with fire pits
- When to Go Based on Your Interests

| Interest | Best Season | Locations |
| --- | --- | --- |
| Snorkeling / Diving | Summer (Dec–Feb) | Great Barrier Reef, Ningaloo Reef |
| Wildlife Watching | Winter (Jun–Aug) | Kangaroo Island, Tasmania, Outback |
| Festivals & City Events | Summer | Sydney, Melbourne |
| Hiking | Winter (cooler & safer) | Uluru, Tasmania, Blue Mountains |
| Skiing | Winter | Snowy Mountains, Victoria Alps |

Travel Tips

- **Flights:** Domestic airfare spikes around school holidays (December–January and June–July). Book early.
- **Packing:** Australia's weather can flip quickly. Even in summer, southern cities like Melbourne can turn cold. In winter, deserts get hot by day and freezing at night.
- **Costs:** Peak-season accommodations (school holidays and Christmas) can jump by 30–50%. Winter in remote regions tends to be cheaper except for ski resorts.

**Bottom Line:**

If you're dreaming of tropical beaches, vibrant events, and reef swims, go in summer. For hiking, wildlife encounters, and cooler temperatures, winter is your season. Both times offer rich, unforgettable experiences—you just need to match the journey to your pace and personality.

# 8.5 Budget Planning, Tour Options, and Travel Apps

Planning your dream trip to Australia doesn't have to be a budget-breaker. With a little foresight, smart use of travel tools, and an understanding of available tour options, you can stretch your dollar and still get the full experience—whether you're traveling solo, with a partner, or as a family.

Understanding Your Budget

Start by setting your overall budget. Australia is known for its high quality of life, and that comfort comes at a cost. On average, backpackers can get by on AUD $70–$100 per day, mid-range travelers should plan for AUD $150–$250, while luxury travelers often spend upwards of AUD $400 per day.

**Typical Daily Expenses Breakdown:**

- **Accommodation:**

  - Hostels: AUD $30–$60 per night (shared room)
  - Mid-range hotels/motels: AUD $120–$180 per night
  - Apartments: AUD $100–$200 (self-contained, often cheaper for longer stays)
  - Campgrounds: AUD $10–$50 (depending on location and amenities)
- **Food & Drink:**

  - Pub meal or café brunch: AUD $15–$25
  - Fast food: AUD $10–$15
  - Dinner at a mid-range restaurant: AUD $25–$50
  - Groceries for DIY meals: ~AUD $60–$100/week
- **Transport:**

  - Public transport: AUD $2.50–$5 per ride (with daily/weekly caps)
  - Car hire: AUD $60–$100 per day (plus petrol)
  - Domestic flights: AUD $80–$250 (book ahead for savings)

- **Attractions & Tours:**

  - Great Barrier Reef snorkeling trip: ~AUD $180–$250
  - Sydney BridgeClimb: AUD $340+
  - Wildlife park entry: AUD $20–$40
  - National Park Passes: AUD $20–$50 depending on the region

A 2-week mid-range trip for two people can run between AUD $4,000–$6,000 with a mix of self-guided and organized activities.

Tour Options: Self-Guided, Group, and Day Tours

Australia offers a healthy mix of DIY and guided travel experiences.

### 1. Self-Guided Adventures
Ideal for confident travelers who enjoy flexibility. Rent a car or campervan and explore at your own pace. National parks, coastal towns are all accessible by self-drive. Use apps like *Wikicamps* to find free or low-cost camping spots and *Google Maps* offline features to stay on track in remote areas.

### 2. Small Group Tours
Best for solo travelers or anyone looking to meet others and cut through the planning. Tour companies like **Intrepid Travel**, **G Adventures**, and **Topdeck** offer themed multi-day tours—from coastal getaways to Outback expeditions. Costs range from AUD $700 for a 5-day tour to over AUD $3,000 for a 2-week all-inclusive experience.

### 3. Day Tours
These are easy to add to any itinerary without committing to long-term group travel. Think Blue Mountains from Sydney, Great Ocean Road from Melbourne, or snorkeling day trips from Cairns. Prices range from AUD $80–$200 per person, often including transport, guides, and meals.

### Tour Booking Tips:

- Book directly through operator websites or reputable aggregators like **GetYourGuide**, **Viator**, or **Klook**.
- Always compare inclusions—cheaper doesn't always mean better value.
- Read traveler reviews for guide quality and itinerary pace.
- Avoid last-minute peak-season bookings; spots fill up quickly in December–January and June–July.

Best Travel Apps for Australia

Modern travel in Australia is made much easier with the right digital tools. Here's a roundup of the most useful apps to keep on hand:

- **Transport:**

  - *TripView (Sydney)* or *PTV (Melbourne)* – Real-time public transport updates
  - *Uber* or *Ola* – Widely available rideshare apps in major cities
  - *13CABS* – Traditional taxi app (handy in more remote areas)
- **Navigation & Planning:**

  - *Google Maps* – Still essential, but download maps offline for remote areas
  - *Roadtrippers* – Great for planning scenic drives and stops
  - *Fuel Map Australia* – Shows cheapest nearby petrol stations
- **Accommodation:**

  - *Booking.com, Airbnb, Agoda* – For everything from hotels to outback cabins
  - *Wikicamps Australia* – Invaluable for camping and RV travelers
- **Dining & Activities:**

  - *Zomato* or *TheFork* – Restaurant reviews, menus, and reservations
  - *GetYourGuide* or *Klook* – Book tours, entry tickets, and city passes
- **Money & Safety:**

  - *Wise* or *Revolut* – Good for international currency and ATM use
  - *Emergency+* – Official Australian emergency app with GPS location services
  - *TravelSafe* – Local emergency numbers and safety guides

Money-Saving Tips

- **Travel Off-Peak:** April–May and September–November see lower prices but still great weather.
- **Use Free Activities:** Australia is full of natural beauty you can enjoy for free—beaches, parks, and walking trails.
- **Look for Multi-Attraction Passes:** In cities like Sydney or Melbourne, these can save you 30–50% on top attractions.
- **Public BBQs:** Found in most parks and beaches—free to use and great for casual meals.

**Final Tip:** Always plan with flexibility. Australia is vast, so build in buffer days and keep backup ideas ready. With smart budgeting and the right tools, your trip can be both affordable and unforgettable. Whether you're chasing coral reefs, city buzz, or starry Outback nights, there's a way to make it work without stretching your wallet.

# Appendix

## Useful Phrases in Aussie English

Australian English is still English—but not quite the way many travelers are used to hearing it. It's casual, colorful, and full of slang that can feel like another language altogether. This shortlist includes some of the most common Aussie phrases you're likely to encounter while traveling, along with what they mean in plain terms.

Use this as a quick-reference guide so you're not caught off guard when someone offers you a "cuppa" or tells you to "rug up." Australians are friendly and quick to laugh, so even if you get a phrase wrong, you'll rarely be met with anything but a smile.

Common Aussie Phrases & Their Meanings

| Aussie Phrase | Meaning |
| --- | --- |
| G'day | Hello |
| How ya going? | How are you? / How's it going? |
| No worries | It's okay / Don't worry about it |
| Mate | Friend (used widely, even to strangers) |
| Arvo | Afternoon |
| Brekkie | Breakfast |
| Cuppa | Cup of tea or coffee |

| | |
|---|---|
| Ripper | Great! Excellent! |
| Fair dinkum | Genuine, real, true |
| Heaps | A lot / Very (e.g., "heaps good") |
| Ta | Thanks |
| Cheers | Thanks / Goodbye (context-dependent) |
| Servo | Gas station (service station) |
| Bottle-o | Liquor store |
| Thongs | Flip-flops (not underwear) |
| Esky | Cooler / Ice box |
| Lollies | Candy / Sweets |
| Snag | Sausage (usually grilled at a BBQ) |
| Barbie | Barbecue |

| | |
|---|---|
| Ute | Pickup truck (utility vehicle) |
| Bushwalk | Hike |
| Trackie dacks | Sweatpants |
| Bogged | Stuck (usually in sand or mud) |
| Reckon | Think or believe |
| She'll be right | It'll be fine |
| Runners | Sneakers / Athletic shoes |
| Macca's | McDonald's |
| Rug up | Dress warmly |
| Sickie | A day off work due to illness |
| Dodgy | Untrustworthy or suspicious |

Quick Tips on Aussie Communication Style

- Australians are informal, and first names are used early in conversation—even with strangers.
- Humor, especially sarcasm and self-deprecation, is common and often dry.

- Swearing can be casual, but it's best avoided until you understand the setting.
- Directness is appreciated. Avoid being overly formal or stiff.

## Emergency Contacts & Embassy Info

When traveling in Australia, it's important to know where to turn if something goes wrong. Emergency services are reliable and responsive, and embassies across the country can assist with lost passports, legal trouble, or urgent support.

Emergency Services (Nationwide)

- **Triple Zero (000)**
  This is Australia's main emergency number. Call 000 for:
  - Police
  - Fire
  - Ambulance

The line operates 24/7 from any phone (mobile or landline) and is free to call. You will be asked to state your emergency and your location.

If you're using a mobile and can't get through on 000, you can try:

- **112** – This number also connects to emergency services and works on all GSM mobile networks, even without signal from your provider.

Health Advice and Non-Urgent Help

- **Healthdirect Australia:** 1800 022 222
  A free government service offering 24/7 health advice from registered nurses.

- **Poisons Information Centre:** 13 11 26
  Available 24/7 for poisoning advice and treatment information.

- **Lifeline (Mental Health):** 13 11 14
  24/7 crisis support and suicide prevention services.

Embassy & Consulate Information

Australia hosts embassies and consulates for most major countries, primarily in **Canberra** (the capital), with additional consulates in cities like **Sydney**, **Melbourne**, **Brisbane**, and **Perth**.

Below are the contact details for a few of the most commonly referenced embassies:

United States

- **Embassy (Canberra):**
  Moonah Place, Yarralumla ACT 2600
  Phone: +61 2 6214 5600
  Website: au.usembassy.gov

- **Consulates:** Sydney, Melbourne, Perth

United Kingdom

- **High Commission (Canberra):**
  Commonwealth Avenue, Yarralumla ACT 2600
  Phone: +61 2 6270 6666
  Website: gov.uk/world/australia

- **Consulates:** Sydney, Melbourne, Perth

Canada

- **High Commission (Canberra):**
  Commonwealth Avenue, Canberra ACT 2600
  Phone: +61 2 6270 4000
  Website: international.gc.ca

- **Consulates:** Sydney

India

- **High Commission (Canberra):**
  3 Moonah Place, Yarralumla ACT 2600
  Phone: +61 2 6273 3999
  Website: hci.canberra.gov.in

- **Consulates:** Sydney, Melbourne, Perth

Tip:

If your country is not listed above, you can find your embassy's contact details through the [Department of Foreign Affairs and Trade (DFAT)](#) or search "Embassy of [Country] in Australia."

2m7

SOUTH AUSTRALIA

Printed in Dunstable, United Kingdom